Croatia

Croatia

MICHAEL A. SCHUMAN

Facts On File, Inc.

Nations in Transition: Croatia

Copyright © 2004 by Michael A. Schuman

Facts On File, Inc.
132 West 31st Street
New York NY 10001

Library of Congress Cataloging-in-Publication Data

Schuman, Michael.
    Croatia / Michael A. Schuman.
        p. cm. — (Nations in transition)
    Includes bibliographical references and index.
    ISBN 0-8160-5053-8
    1. Croatia. I. Title. II. Series.
    DR1510.S37 2003
    949.72—dc21   2003049188

Facts On File books are available at special discounts when purchased in bulk quantities for businesses, associations, institutions, or sales promotions. Please call our Special Sales Department in New York at (212) 967-8800 or (800) 322-8755.

You can find Facts On File on the World Wide Web at
http://www.factsonfile.com

Text design by Erika K. Arroyo
Cover design by Nora Wertz
Map by Patricia Meschino © Facts On File

Printed in the United States of America

MP JT 10 9 8 7 6 5 4 3 2 1

This book is printed on acid-free paper.

CONTENTS

INTRODUCTION

If one was to play a word association game with the name *Croatia*, one would likely hear a wide array of responses, depending greatly on who gave the reply.

For example, any person who followed the news during the early to mid-1990s would likely respond with the word *victim*. To people who lived during World War II, 1939–45, the answer would be along the lines of *oppressor*. To others, depending on their interests, personal views, and expertise, possible comebacks could be *Slavic, mountains, beaches, Yugoslavia, communist,* and *basketball*. For a nation that is a little smaller than the state of West Virginia, with a population of only 4.6 million people, Croatia is a colorful land with a long, strange heritage.

Croatia, officially called the Republic of Croatia (Republika Hrvatska in the native tongue), dates back 1,500 years and has been at times an independent kingdom, a part of Hungary, a part of Austria and Hungary, a part of a united kingdom with other Balkan peoples, a part of a fascist dictatorship, a part of a maverick communist entity, and an independent democracy. The Croat leadership massacred Serbs, Jews, Roma (Gypsies), and other minorities by actively siding with the Nazis during World War II, yet they themselves were victimized by Serbs in the 1990s. Croatia's mixed history has influenced who Croats are today.

Geography

Croatia is an odd-looking nation, shaped somewhat like a crescent. Some think it resembles the mouth of an alligator, ready to swallow Bosnia and Herzegovina, the country it almost completely surrounds.

To the northwest, Croatia borders Slovenia, which was once, along with Croatia, part of Yugoslavia, to the northeast it borders Hungary. Due east, a bit of Croatia abuts Serbia, while to the south a small fringe shares a border with Montenegro. (Serbia and Montenegro, both former republics of Yugoslavia, today are independent nations.) Western Croatia rests against the Adriatic Sea; across the Adriatic from Croatia is Italy.

If you want to visit a country with breathtaking scenery, Croatia is the place to go. Geographically, as well as historically, the republic is usually divided into three sections. Running the length of the eastern arm of the nation is the Pannonian Plain, also known as Croatia-Slavonia or simply Slavonia. In prehistory, it was the site of what is today referred to by geologists as the Pannonian Sea. This is Croatia's breadbasket. Wheat, corn, barley, oats, potatoes, sugar beets, beans, and other produce grow in abundance here, thanks to the alluvial soil deposited by the Drava River, near the Serbia border, and the Sava River, which flows through north-central Croatia.

Mountains rise in isolated parts of the plain. North of the republic's capital of Zagreb, in the north central part of the plain, are the Medvednica Mountains. Also on the Pannonian Plain are two other small ranges: the Papuk Mountains, and south of them, the Psunj Mountains.

The climate in the Pannonian Plain is similar to the rest of central Europe, with hot summers and cold winters. Temperatures in the region have gotten above 100°F in summer and below 0°F in winter, but generally range in the 80s in summer and the mid-20s to mid-30s in winter.

West of the Pannonian region is a mountain belt that is part of the Dinaric Alps, which roughly parallel the Adriatic Sea. Smaller chains of the Dinaric Alps in Croatia include the Velika Kapela Mountains, stretching south from the southwestern border with Slovenia, the Plješevica Mountains, along the border with Bosnia and Herzegovina, and the Velebit Mountains, along the Adriatic Sea. The highest peak is Mount Troglav, which at 6,276 feet is taller than the peaks in the Appalachian Mountains in the United States but considerably lower than the Rockies. Croatia's mountains generally are heavily forested at their bases, with vegetation gradually decreasing until it all but disappears at the summits. The land in this region is mostly worthless for growing any produce, although some isolated meadows are farmed.

Any person venturing into the mountains in winter can expect to find a lot of snow on the ground and cold temperatures, typically in the low 20s. Heavy rains are common in early summer, with mild temperatures in the 60s.

Another geographic region constitutes Croatia's long and glorious coastline, which has welcomed seafarers for centuries. The seacoast is actually composed of two distinct parts. The first is the little triangle-shaped Istrian Peninsula, which dangles like a pendant off the republic's far northwestern corner. The other is the long coastal stretch known historically as Dalmatia. (Yes, the Dalmatian dog is named for the region and is believed to have originated there.)

Dalmatia stretches over 1,100 miles. Off the coastline are more than 1,000 islands, making this the largest archipelago, or chain of islands, in Europe. What the region lacks in arable land it makes up for with its beaches, which, despite being more rocky than sandy, are among the most popular in eastern Europe. Dry, cold northerly winds known as mistral winds moderate the temperatures along the coast. The thermometer rarely dips below freezing in winter and usually falls in the 60s and 70s in summer. Rain falls mostly in winter and rarely in summer, making ideal conditions for beach vacationers.

Inland Water

There are 26 rivers of moderate to large size flowing at least 30 miles within Croatia. The most important are the Drava and Sava on the Pannonian Plain. Both rivers form borders between Croatia and a neighboring country. The Drava begins in Austria, enters Croatia from Slovenia, and forms much of the border between Croatia and Hungary. The Sava has its source in Slovenia. Croatia's capital, Zagreb, sits alongside the Sava, which flows on to form most of the boundary of Croatia and Bosnia and Herzegovina. Two of the Sava's tributaries are the Kupa and Una Rivers, found in central Croatia.

The other major river in the republic is the Neretva, which has its source in Bosnia and Herzegovina and empties into the Adriatic. The Neretva is a rarity. Most of Croatia's rivers flow eastward out of Croatia, ending at the Black Sea. Two others which do flow into the Adriatic are Dalmatia's Krka and Cetina Rivers, noteworthy for their hydroelectric possibilities. The fact that Croatia's major rivers flow through other countries has always been convenient for foreign trade.

Plitvice Lakes, one of the seven national parks in Croatia, consists of 16 lakes connected by numerous waterfalls. (Courtesy Croatian National Tourist Office, New York)

Croatia is not well known for lakes, but among 16 of the world's most spectacular ones are the Plitvice Lakes in the mountains in the republic's western arc. Together they form Plitvice Lakes National Park, declared in 1949. In 1979, the United Nations Educational, Scientific and Cultural Organization (UNESCO) placed the park on its World Heritage List, designating it a place of unusual beauty that must be protected. The lakes are as clear as glass and known for their myriad cascades and waterfalls. Combined boat-and-bus tours allow tourists to enjoy the grandeur of these rare bodies of water. Unfortunately, the area was held by the Serbs during the Balkan war from 1991 to 1995, and land mines were planted throughout the area. Observers say that land mines are still scattered throughout the region.

Money and Language

When Croatia declared itself an independent republic in 1991, its central bank issued its own currency, the Croatian dinar, but it was never meant to be a permanent one. On May 30, 1994, the dinar was replaced with a kuna, which is divisible into 100 lipas. The kuna takes its name from a small animal called a marten, similar to a ferret or mink. The marten's pelt was traded as a form of currency in Roman times, and a coin called a kuna was first used in the 1200s.

Croatia's official language is a south Slavic tongue simply called Croatian. It is very similar to languages spoken in neighboring countries, especially Serbian. One major difference is that Croatian is written in Roman script, as is English, while Serbian is usually written in Cyrillic.

Many letters in Croatian are pronounced the same as in English, but there are exceptions. The letter s with a haček above it (š) is pronounced "sh." The letter j is pronounced like "y," and c with either a haček (č) or an acute accent (ć) above it is pronounced as "ch." The letter ž is pronounced like "zh" or a hard "jh."

While Croatian is the primary language in the Republic of Croatia, it is hardly the nation's only spoken language. The unofficial language of the tourist industry is German, spoken mainly to accommodate the many German-speaking people who visit. Because of their proximity to Italy, residents of the peninsula of Istria favor Italian, and there is a smattering of English spoken, especially among young people.

National Symbols

The Republic of Croatia's flag consists of three horizontal, rectangular stripes: red at the top, white in the middle, and blue on the bottom. The stripes' lengths are twice their width, and each occupies one-third of the flag's space. The colors represent Croatian national unity. In the 1830s and 1840s the Illyrian movement, a nationalistic political trend, swept Croatia. Activists in the movement wore jackets decorated in red, white, and blue. One of the movement's heroes, Viceroy Josip Jelačić, wore a uniform in those same colors when sworn into office in 1848.

In the center of the flag is Croatia's historical coat of arms, which takes the shape of a shield. The upper part of the coat of arms, the crown, rests on the bottom part of the red stripe on the flag. Most of the body of the coat of arms sits across the middle of the white stripe, while the symbol's lowest part overlaps the center of the blue stripe.

The crown in the coat of arms is divided into five smaller coats of arms, which also take the shapes of shields. From left to right they are the oldest known Croatian coat of arms, which is a yellow six-pointed star and a white crescent moon on a blue shield. Next there are coats of arms of the four official geographic sections of Croatia: the Dubrovnik Republic, Dalmatia, Istria, and Slavonia. The main body of the coat of arms is a checkerboard of 25 alternating red and white squares. The current Croatian coat of arms is known to date to about 1508 or 1512, but might be older.

The National Anthem

Croatia's national anthem is titled *Lijepa naša domovino* (Our beautiful homeland). Its words were written by Croatian poet Antun Mihanović and were first printed in a magazine called *Danica* (The morning star) in 1835. Croatian songwriter Josip Runjanin put Mihanović's verses to music in 1846, and the song debuted as the national anthem at an economics convention in 1891. Its lyrics, translated into English, follow:

Our Beautiful Homeland

Beautiful is our homeland,
O so fearless, o so gracious,
Our fathers' ancient glory,
May God bless you, live forever!

You are our only glory
You are our only treasure,
Yes, we love your plains and valleys,
Yes, we love your hills and mountains.

Sava, Drava, keep on flowing,
Danube, do not lose your vigor,
Deep blue sea go tell the whole world,
That a Croat loves his homeland.

When his fields are kissed by sunshine,
When his oaks are whipped by wild winds,
When his dear ones go to heaven,
Still his heart beats for Croatia!

NOTE

pp. xii–xiii "Our Beautiful Homeland." "The National Anthem of Croatia," Discover Beautiful Croatia home page. Available on-line. URL: http://www.romwell.com/travel/advisory/europe/croatia/himna.html. Downloaded on February 12, 2003.

PART I

History

1

PREHISTORY TO EARLY 1910s

Today it is known as Croatia, but until around 1,000 B.C. this land with so much rich history was nothing but a wilderness of forests, plains, hills, and barren, rocky mountains. The region's original inhabitants were members of tribes who emigrated from other parts of Europe and Asia. The general region of what is today southeastern Europe was then known by the name Illyria.

Life in Illyria

The people who lived here, the Illyrians, an Indo-European people, were a tough and warlike group. Much of the time they were involved in war or piracy against their neighbors. When not on the attack, they carved out a society in which they survived by raising wheat and hunting fish and game. They also crafted practical items such as pottery, clothing, and weapons. Evidence has shown that the Illyrians took time to make decorations, too, mainly out of iron and copper. The Illyrians traded cattle or manufactured goods with neighboring tribes to get items they did not grow or make.

The mighty and legendary Greek Empire was at the peak of its power by around 400 B.C. The Greeks invaded and conquered much of Illyria under Philip II (359–336), including what is now Croatia, and called the inhabitants Paeonii. About a hundred years after the Greeks established themselves here, Celtic tribes moved down from what are now the British Isles into the same territory.

In the 300s B.C., the Roman Empire, based west of Greece, emerged as a major military power, and in the following three centuries the Romans conquered the vast Greek territory. They also made inroads north into the European continent, including an area called Dalmatia, a two-hundred-mile-long strip of land on the Adriatic coastline, now part of the modern republic of Croatia.

When residents of Dalmatia battled the Romans in 35 B.C., its neighbors fought on their side. The Romans under Emperor Augustus took on nearly all of Illyria and by 9 B.C. had conquered and occupied it. They gave a permanent name to the land that would become part of Croatia: Pannonia, after the Greek term *Paeonii*. Pannonia was turned into a full-fledged province of the Roman Empire.

The Roman Empire took advantage of the Pannonians' reputation and recruited many of their best soldiers from the province. Some, such as Trajan Decius, Aurelian, and Diocletian matured into some of the Roman Empire's most competent generals. Rome had a stranglehold on the area until cracks in the empire started to appear in the late fourth century A.D. In A.D. 395 the crumbling Roman Empire abandoned Pannonia.

To fill the vacuum left by the Romans, other groups settled into the area. A large number are believed to have been pagans from the region of present day Ukraine and eastern Russia.

THE TOUGH PANNONIANS

The warlike Pannonians became known as some of the toughest people in the Roman Empire. To this day people in central Europe associate the name *Pannonia* with power. For example, a motorcycle manufacturer in the modern nation of Hungary, also once part of the same Roman province, introduced its mightiest model in 1954; to reflect the motorcycle's strength, the company named it the Pannonia.

Other historians say the Croats' ancestors were a tribe called the Sarmatians, who moved from Central Asia. The scholars who believe the Sarmatian theory say this tribe overtook the tribal Slavs living in central Europe and formed their own small state in today's Poland they called White Croatia. Eventually these White Croats intermarried with other Slavs, who took the name Croats to describe themselves.

While the western territories of the Roman Empire fell, its eastern part continued to thrive as the Byzantine Empire. It was named after the ancient Greek city Byzantium, located on the Bosporus Strait, which connects the Black and Mediterranean Seas, where Europe meets Asia. In A.D. 330, the Roman emperor Constantine the Great moved the capital of the Roman Empire from Rome to Byzantium. The city was renamed Constantinople after him. Today the site of Constantinople is occupied by Istanbul, Turkey.

Constantine helped the spread of Christianity when he converted to that religion. This eastern form of Christianity is now known as Orthodox Christianity.

A 10th-century Byzantine historian wrote that the Byzantine emperor teamed up his forces with the White Croats to invade Dalmatia in the 600s. Their goal was to boot out the remaining Slavs and another tribe called the Avars. Once that was accomplished, the White Croats settled in Dalmatia. Meanwhile, two other groups of Slavs calling themselves Croats became entrenched in other regions of southeastern Europe. A group called the Red Croats lived mainly in modern day Montenegro, to the south. Another one, based along the Sava River in present day north-central Croatia, became known as the Pannonian Croats.

The Influence of Charlemagne

In the late 700s, the Franks, a Germanic people, conquered the Croats. The Franks' leader, the renowned Charlemagne (ca. 742–814), ruled the lands of the Croats as a suzerainty, meaning he controlled their relations with other nations but allowed them to make their own domestic decisions. In A.D. 803, the Croatian tribes formally accepted the rule of Charlemagne.

One major effect of life under Charlemagne was the Croats' change in religious beliefs. Charlemagne was a Catholic Christian and he sent

In 803, the tribes in present day Croatia formally accepted the rule of Charlemagne, depicted here crossing the Alps. (Courtesy Free Library of Philadelphia)

missionaries to convert his subjects to his religion. By the mid-800s, nearly all the Croatians had become Catholics. The main exception was the area around Dalmatia, which continued under the rule of the Orthodox Church of the Byzantine Empire.

The varied Croatian tribes living along the Adriatic coastline (the former Roman republic of Dalmatia) and in an area called Slavonia (mainly the former Roman republic of Pannonia) organized separate states for themselves in the late 870s. Between 910 and 914 the leader of Croatian Dalmatia, Tomislav (r. 910–ca. 929) united his Croatian state with Slavonia. Then in 924 or 925, a representative of Pope John X crowned Tomislav the first king of the Croats. With the Byzantine Empire losing power, officials of the Catholic Church of the Croats decided to take advantage of that situation. They cut all ties between the Croats and the Orthodox Church.

Over roughly the next 180 years, the Croatian state engaged in several battles and skirmishes with the Byzantine Empire over possession of Adriatic seaports. The most important among them was the beautiful and walled city of Dubrovnik, which changed hands several times. Despite the fact that the region was unstable, the Croatian kingdom was at its most powerful during the 1000s. That came to a crashing halt in 1089, when Croatian king Zvonimir (r. 1075–89) died without any heirs.

The Croat kingdom was in chaos. For two years the nobles of Croatia fought among themselves over who should lead the kingdom. Neighboring Hungary, north of the Croatian kingdom, took advantage of the infighting by invading and conquering the Croats in 1091. Hungary's King Laszlo I (r. 1077–95) (also known as King Ladislaus I), established a bishopric, or territory of a Catholic bishop, in the Croatian city of Zagreb. Not long after Laszlo's death, King Kalman (r. 1095–1114) succeeded him on the throne.

This artwork depicts King Tomislav, who united his Croatian state with Slavonia, some time between 910 and 914. (Courtesy Free Library of Philadelphia)

A Noted Agreement

In 1102, Kalman and Croatian tribal chiefs signed an agreement called the Pacta Conventa, which in Latin means simply "the conditions agreed on." This became one of the most important documents in the history of the Croatian people, for the Pacta Conventa was the basis for the close relationship between Hungary and the Croats for more than 800 years.

Under the pact, Croatia had its own local governor, known by the title *ban*. It also had its own assembly of nobles, called the Sabor. In addition, the Croats maintained their own army.

However, the basic meaning of the agreement was interpreted differently by many Hungarians and Croats for centuries. The Croats insisted that while both peoples would share one king, Croatia would be a sovereign state with autonomy, or self-rule. At the same time, the Hungarians believed that with the signing of the Pacta Conventa they fully annexed Croatia in 1102.

Those misinterpretations led to some uneven ways of governing the kingdom. Some Hungarian kings did truly try to absorb Croatia into Hungary. On other occasions the Croats selected and lived under their own king. As a result of battles and political disagreements, the borders of Croatia and Hungary often changed. Regardless of who was governing whom at any time, the fact is that Hungarian culture became much of the way of life for the Croats. Perhaps the most dominant part of Hungarian lifestyle of the period to enter the Croats' day-to-day existence was feudalism.

With its increased size and power, the Kingdom of Hungary was anxious to keep its hands on Dalmatia. Landlocked Hungary needed a seaport for trade, but Dalmatia was a much coveted area. Venice, at the time a city-state that included much of northeastern Italy and important Mediterranean islands such as Crete and Cyprus, also wanted Dalmatia. There were hardwood trees growing in the forests of the strategic coastal area, and the doges, or rulers of Venice, wanted that timber to construct trading ships. Venice had numerous trade routes throughout the Mediterranean region.

The result was constant warfare between Hungary and Venice over Dalmatia. Naturally, the biggest victims of these squabbles were the Dalmatians. Between 1115 and 1420, 21 wars were fought between Hungary

FEUDALISM

For more than 500 years, life in Europe was governed by a system called feudalism. The word *feudal* comes from a Latin term for the word *fief,* which was the expanse of land owned by a lord and run by his subjects.

The social, economic, and military system of feudalism dominated Europe from around the 700s well into the 1300s. The system worked as follows. A lord owned a fief, which ranged in size from a fairly small parcel of property to a huge province of a kingdom. The lord granted the use of the land to his subjects, called vassals, who like the lord were aristocrats. No peasants were permitted to take part in this system. A common maxim of the day was, "No land without a lord, and no lord without a land."

The lord and his vassals bound their agreements through rituals and ceremonies. The observance in which a man became a vassal was called *homage.* During the ritual the new vassal promised to be a loyal fighter for the lord, and the lord promised to treat his vassal with honor. Homage was usually followed by a ceremony called *investiture,* where the lord gave the rights of his fief to the vassal. Much of the time the investiture was sealed by the lord giving the vassal a clump of earth, a tree branch, or some other symbol of the land.

Although the lord still owned the land, the vassal was allowed its use. Of course, the vassal did not usually do the physical labor on the fief. That work was left to peasants, who were allowed to live on the land under the protection of the lord. The vassal would receive whatever crops the peasants produced, and it was up to the vassal to manage the peasants' work, reward them for their labor, and mete out justice.

Vassals also were responsible for protection of the fief. For that purpose vassals supplied knights, or warriors on horseback, to serve the lord for specified periods of time, commonly 40 days. These were the knights of legend who protected themselves by wearing metal armor. By the later years of feudalism, vassals subdivided their fiefs and parceled out sections to their knights, who in turn became vassals.

The system of feudalism began to decline in the 1200s. One reason was that soldiers began to be paid for their services, so lords no longer had to rely on vassals for protection. Another reason was the invention of gunpowder, which pierced armor, thereby making the knights' metal protection useless. As the cities and towns of Europe grew, people started to be paid for providing the same work vassals had been doing on lords' fiefs.

Feudalism peaked from the 800s to the 1200s. By the 1400s the system had all but disappeared from the European landscape.

and Venice over Dalmatia, and Dalmatian cities such as Split and Dubrovnik (Ragusa) changed hands numerous times. Finally, in 1420, the Venetians established rule over all of Dalmatia, which they would control for nearly 400 years.

Under the Ottoman Turks

While the Byzantine Empire had disintegrated, another power took its place in the same region. This was the empire of the Ottoman Turks, also centered around Istanbul. By the 1300s the Ottomans, who were Muslims, were increasing their territory in every direction. The city of Dubrovnik recognized the growing influence of the Ottomans and in that century became the first Christian-based government to establish relations with them. Dubrovnik in fact thrived by becoming a prime trading partner with the Ottomans, sending them everything from precious gems to slaves. Dubrovnik also became a leading mediator between the Ottomans and the European republics.

It turned out that the leaders of Dubrovnik were foresighted to get on the good side of the Ottomans. By the mid-1500s, the Ottomans conquered nearly all of Croatia south and east of the Sava River. The turning point came in 1526 at the Battle of Mohács in Hungary, where the Ottoman Turks under the command of Sultan Suleiman (Sulëyman) I (1494–1566) overran the Hungarian army led by King Louis II (1506–26).

Everything changed as a result of the battle. Hungary no longer existed as a kingdom. What was once the Croatian section of Hungary was divided into Hapsburg and Ottoman territories. János (John) Zapolya (1540–71), later John II, king of Hungary, ultimately led the Ottoman section, and the Hapsburg king Ferdinand I of Austria (1503–1564), later Holy Roman Emperor, governed the Hapsburg part of Croatia. The Austrian leader tightened his grip on the Croatians. First, he reduced the power of the Croatians' body of government, the Sabor. Then he set up a military border across Croatia.

Ferdinand recruited peasants from throughout the Hapsburg Empire, including Germans, Hungarians, Serbs, and other Slavs to guard the borders from invasions. To make the job of border guard seem more appealing, he gave local independence and land to those agreeing to take the

THE BATTLE OF MOHÁCS

Suleiman the Magnificent is recognized by historians as most likely the strongest sultan in the lengthy history of the Ottoman Empire. Suleiman did not think it was necessary to add Hungary to his massive empire. He simply wanted the small European kingdom to be on his side. To the north of Hungary was another mighty military power: the Hapsburg Empire, which ruled much of central Europe. Suleiman wanted Hungary to be a buffer between his empire and the Hapsburgs.

His opponent was a 20-year-old sickly young man named Louis (Lazslo) II, the king of Hungary. Louis did not want any trouble with the Ottomans. He knew they had been guilty of raiding and pillaging enemies.

However, Louis's wife, Queen Maria, was the sister of the king of Austria, and Austria was part of the Hapsburg Empire. In addition, Hungary was a Christian nation and did not want to be controlled by Muslims.

As Louis mulled over the decision, Suleiman took matters into his own hands, and at around 2 P.M. on August 29, 1526, he invaded Hungary. He had with him 70,000 to 80,000 troops as well as supply men pulling wagons and leading camels. Among the soldiers was a group of janissaries, the elite corps of the Ottoman army and a highly effective military force.

The battle took place on a large barren field extending to a small, flat hill. It is believed that Louis's army consisted of from 30,000 to 50,000 troops, including all ranks, from knights to peasants. While Louis and his men approached the field, Suleiman's troops charged down the slopes on the Hungarians' right side. Louis and his warriors overwhelmed and crushed Suleiman's advance troops.

However, right behind this vanguard were the Ottomans' main forces, which included the feared janissaries. Suleiman's engineers had cut special paths on the muddy slopes just for the use of the janissaries. Suleiman's bigger and better trained forces ran roughshod over the Hungarians. It is estimated that about 18,000 Hungarians and Ottomans died in the battle, which was finished just four hours after it had started. Suleiman gathered any of the surviving Hapsburg troops he could find and slashed their necks, cutting off their heads.

Louis survived the battle but was thrown from his horse into a nearby stream. He drowned in his heavy and clunky metal armor.

dangerous occupation and live on the border. He also awarded Orthodox Christians freedom of religion, although the Catholic Church mightily opposed it.

At that time the Catholic Church was undergoing some major difficulties. The Protestant Reformation was sweeping through much of Europe. Led by German religious leader Martin Luther, the goal of this movement was to reform the Catholic Church.

Croatia was not spared from this religious tumult. Among those welcoming forms of non-Catholic Christianity were some of the most important landowning nobles. Then, in 1562, two Croats named Stipan Konzul and Anton Dalmatin published the first Croatian Bible.

This anti-Catholic fervor did not last long. In 1609, the Sabor voted to ban any religion other than Catholicism in Croatia, and some of the same nobles who had converted and become Protestants converted back to the Catholic faith. This period, known as the Counterreformation, led to a flourishing of Catholicism in the Hapsburg portion of Croatia. One order of the Catholic Church, called the Jesuits, established schools and wrote a Croatian dictionary, grammar books, and religious books to aid in teaching young people. This was the beginning of the foundation of Croatian literature. Meanwhile, another order of Catholics called the Franciscans went into the Ottoman portions of Croatia in an attempt to convert resident Muslims to Christianity.

In 1683, the Turks began a siege around the Austrian capital city of Vienna. The Hapsburgs successfully defended the city, beginning a lengthy war between the Hapsburgs and the Ottomans that ended in a Hapsburg victory in 1697. In 1699, nearly all of Croatia, as well as other European lands including Hungary and Slavonia, was ceded to Austria. According to many historians, the treaty "marked the beginning of the Ottoman Empire's disintegration."

The Powerful Hapsburgs

In the 1700s, the Hapsburgs gained more and more European territory, concentrating their government in Vienna. In 1765, Emperor Joseph II, known as the Enlightened Emperor, took control of the Hapsburg throne and by the 1780s made major efforts to modernize the lands under his control. One such decision was to rule the empire with a strong, central government in Vienna. Another was to select one language as the official one of the empire. Joseph chose German and immediately angered both the Hungarians and the Croats by doing so.

The Hungarians were devoted to their national language, Magyar. While they did not want it to be the language of the entire empire, they wanted it at least to be the official language of Hungary. The Croats were concerned about losing their national identity to both the Austrians and Hungarians and favored keeping Latin as the language of the empire. Rebellion was on the horizon.

Joseph II died in 1790, and his successor, Leopold II, made immediate changes in order to ease tensions. He dropped the idea of a dominant central government. He also tossed aside the idea of an official language for the whole empire. Leopold signed laws that made certain that Hungary would be recognized as an independent kingdom under the Hapsburg emperor.

To the west, the young French general Napoleon rose to power as part of a movement to change France from a monarchy to a democratic republic. The movement led to the French Revolution, fought over 10 years, which introduced democratic standards in the French government and gave the middle class a stronger say in its leadership.

Once Napoleon became emperor in 1804, he went on a spree to conquer much of western and central Europe and place it under French control. The Venetian Republic had been weakening for some time, and Napoleon put the last nail in the coffin. In 1809, he captured Dalmatia and Dubrovnik on the Adriatic coast and gained a foothold in western Croatia. Together, these conquered lands became known as the French Illyrian Provinces.

The French leadership took an active role in strengthening the standard of living in the Illyrian Provinces. They helped boost commerce and agriculture and also aggressively fought piracy, a serious threat at the time. French rule did not last long, though. After a disastrous defeat in Russia, Napoleon was forced to retreat. The Illyrian Provinces were regained by the Hapsburgs; Dalmatia was retaken by Austria; and Croatia again became part of Hungary. In 1816, Austria converted the Illyrian Provinces into the Kingdom of Illyria.

One long-term effect of the French Revolution was a substantial increase in nationalism in much of Europe. This feeling extended into Croatia.

By the 1830s, Croats began showing some independence by promoting the Croatian tongue. In 1832, for the first time in hundreds of years, a Croatian noble spoke to the Sabor in his native language. Croats took their push for independence further when in 1836 a journalist named Ljudevit Gaj began publishing an anti-Hungarian journal calling for Illyrian independence.

That sent shock waves through the Hungarian leadership. They banned the word *Illyria* from public speech but were unable to stop the growth of the movement for Illyrian unity. In 1843, the Hungarian government voted to make Magyar the official language of Hungarian-Croatian political relations. The Croats were outraged, saying the law violated their rights as a separate people. They lobbied the Hapsburg leadership in Vienna for separation from Hungary. When the Hungarian assembly sent official documents written in Magyar, the Croats returned them.

Hence, when the Hungarians rose up against Austria in 1848, the Croats were on Austria's side. Croatia's ultimate goal was a union including Dalmatia and Slavonia. Croatia's ban Josip Jelačić (1801–1859) headed a military force that attacked Hungary's army. Jelačić was a soldier of limited abilities, and his troops withdrew with little success, but an invasion by the Russians into Hungary forced an end to the Hungarian Revolution.

Although the Croats had fought with the winners, the Austrians did little to reward them for their support. Now suspicious of all entities of the empire, Austria ruled its lands with an iron fist. The government became even more greatly centralized under Vienna's rule and made Germanization a cultural hallmark. The Slavic union of Croatia, Slavonia, and Dalmatia that Jelačić had lobbied for did not take place. The only gain for the Croats was an end to serfdom, or the feudal system, in which workers were bound for life to a wealthy landowner.

The 1860s brought a quick weakening of the Hapsburg Empire. In 1866, the empire lost the Battle of Königgrätz to the potent Germanic nation of Prussia in north-central Europe, which fought under the formi-

Croat laborers gather in 1855, when Croatia was under Austrian rule. During this period, serfdom in Croatia ended. (Courtesy Library of Congress)

dable might of its chancellor, Otto von Bismarck (1815–1898). The breakup of Austria's realm had begun. In 1867, Hungary became a kingdom in its own right but was united with Austria under the single leadership of Austrian emperor Francis Joseph (1830–1916). This unusual cooperation became known as both the Dual Monarchy and the nation of Austria-Hungary.

The Croatian dream of a unified Slavic country was still unrealized. Dalmatia was part of Austria, while Croatia and Slovenia still belonged to Hungary. In 1868, the Sabor adopted a compromise agreement, the Nagodba. It gave Croatia limited autonomy. Croatia no longer needed approval from either Vienna or the Hungarian capital of Budapest to decide on purely internal matters, including its education system, but for decisions on financial matters, the Nagodba required consent from Vienna and Budapest. While Hungary's government felt the Croats should be grateful for the freedoms that were given under the Nagodba, Croatia felt it was a sham. A law was passed soon afterward that assured pro-Hungarian officials a majority in the Sabor.

Living under the leadership of a dual monarchy led to a lot of confusion for those both inside and outside the Balkans. James Joyce, a writer from Ireland who at that time was teaching in Istria, the peninsula now occupied by Croatia and Slovenia, wrote of the political situation, "I hate this Catholic country with its hundred races and thousand languages, governed by a parliament which can transact no business and sits for a week at the most and by the most physically corrupt house in Europe."

This view highlights the eternal city of Ragusa, now Dubrovnik, some time between 1890 and 1900. (Courtesy Library of Congress)

Corrupt or not, Austria-Hungary ruled Croatia over most of the next four decades. While Croatian enmity toward Austria-Hungary continued, the Croats soon began battling among themselves. Two distinct political factions of Croats developed. One, led by Bishop Josip Strossmayer (1815–1905), favored a union of all southern Slavs, especially the Croats and Serbs. Strossmayer believed that even though there were major religious differences, with the Serbs mainly Orthodox Christians and the Croats mostly Catholics, the two groups should celebrate their similarities in a show of cultural unity. Strossmayer put his feelings into action when, in 1867, he founded the Yugoslav (meaning "South Slav") Academy of Arts and Sciences.

Opposing Strossmayer were two young nationalists named Ante Starcević (1823–96) and Eugen Kvaternik (1825–71). Both Starčević and Kvaternik wanted a greater Croatia made up of Croatia, Slavonia, Dalmatia, and another Balkan state known as Bosnia and Herzegovina. At the same time, Serbian nationalists promoted their own greater Serbia. They, too, coveted Bosnia and Herzegovina. A fierce rivalry between the Croats and Serbs was the result.

This was a dismal period for Croatia. In 1881, Austria-Hungary extended its military border into Croatia, which caused the population of ethnic Serbs in Croatia to increase to about 2.6 million, or 25 percent of the total population. Serbia was naturally angry, and the rivalry between the Croats and Serbs intensified. The bad times for Croatia peaked when a Hungarian leader Ban Count Dragutin Károly Khuen-Héderváry (1849–1918) gained power in 1883. He was a cruel and uncompromising ruler, who acted as if the Nagodba did not exist and heavily promoted Hungary's national interests in the region. He stayed in power until 1903, when a southern Slav rebellion caused Budapest to remove Khuen-Héderváry from his post.

Unified in their objection to Hungarian rule, the Croats and Serbs worked together to form a political association. In 1908, they won a majority in the Sabor. Hungarian leadership tried forcing apart the new alliance and even resorted to bringing false treason charges against ethnic Serbian leaders in Croatia. These trials on trumped-up charges were brought to the attention of Europe's leaders and only caused the ties between the Serbs and Croats to become stronger in their opposition to Hungary's unbridled power.

NOTES

p. 16 "'I hate this Catholic country . . .'" Stuart Gilbert, editor. *Letters of James Joyce* (London, 1957, p. 57), quoted in Misha Glenny, *The Balkans: Nationalism, War and the Great Powers, 1804–1999.* (New York: Viking Press, 2000), p. 253.

p. 17 "'In 1881, Austria-Hungary extended its military border . . .'" Library of Congress. "Yugoslavia: The Croats and Their Territories." Available on-line. URL: http://lcweb2.loc.gov/cgi-bin/query. Downloaded on November 20, 2002.

2

WORLD WAR I THROUGH THE DEATH OF TITO

Momentum was gaining for a union of Serbs and Croats as the first decade of the 20th century was drawing to a close. However, momentum toward a more ominous future for the Balkans was also brewing. Nationalist tensions were high.

In October 1912, Croatia's neighbor Serbia joined with the nearby countries of Bulgaria, Montenegro, and Greece to invade Turkey, the nation formed from what was left of the Ottoman Empire. The Serbs had dreams of a greater Serbia that would include not only people living within Serbia's borders but also those of Serbian descent residing in Bosnia and Herzegovina. This conflict, known as the First Balkan War, lasted eight months. It ended when a peace treaty was signed in London, England, on May 30, 1913. No longer a mighty empire, the Turks ceded a large swath of their land to the Balkan countries. As a result of the treaty, Serbia and Montenegro became twice their former size, and the new nation of Albania was created between Serbia and the Adriatic Sea.

The peace was an uneasy one. Just a month later another small Balkan war broke out, ending with another treaty, this one signed August 10.

These were tense times in the Balkans, with militant nationalism at odds with longstanding colonialism. Even so, who knew that it would be a teenager who would light the fuse that set off the bomb?

The Day a Teenager Started a World War

One group of extreme nationalists in Serbia was known as the Black Hand. It insisted that Bosnia and Herzegovina belonged to Serbia, not Austria-Hungary. The leader of the Black Hand, Dragutin Dimitrijević, was an officer in the Serbian army.

In the spring of 1914, Dimitrijević heard news that the heir to the throne of Austria-Hungary, Archduke Francis Ferdinand, and his wife, Sophie, planned a visit to Sarajevo on June 28. Dimitrijević dispatched eight members of the Black Hand to Sarajevo with a job to do: murder the archduke and so destroy a symbol of Austro-Hungarian power.

On June 28, the eight plotters positioned themselves in various locations along Appel Quay, one of the biggest streets in Sarajevo and part of the route of the archduke's motorcade. Most of the crowd lining Appel Quay was friendly toward the royal couple, but the congenial atmosphere was broken when one of the would-be assassins tossed a bomb at the archduke's car.

The rest of the assassins scattered, thinking the archduke had been killed. However, Francis Ferdinand had survived the attack and went on to give a scheduled speech at a formal gathering. After that event had ended, Francis Ferdinand and his wife decided to visit victims of the bombing in a nearby hospital. While on the way, the archduke's driver stopped briefly to turn around in front of a grocery store. By chance, one of the assassins, a 19-year-old, sallow-complexioned postman's son and member of the Black Hand named Gavrilo, or Gabriel, Princip (1894–1918), was leaving the store at the same time. Realizing that the archduke was still alive, Princip pulled a gun out of his pocket and fired two shots, killing both Francis Ferdinand and Sophie. (Princip was later sentenced to life in prison but died prematurely of tuberculosis in 1918).

Repercussions of the assassination were felt immediately throughout Europe. Austria-Hungary blamed not just the Black Hand for the murder, but Serbia as a nation. They gave Serbia a 10-point ultimatum and demanded a response within two days.

The Serbs had few problems with most of the points. However, they refused to comply with one: They would not permit Austro-Hungarian officials to actively investigate the assassination on Serbian land. Neither side gave in on this one point, and on July 25, the two countries formally broke off relations with each other. What would become World War I officially began on July 28, when Austria-Hungary declared war on Serbia.

Within days, old alliances between the nations of Europe took hold as they began choosing sides. Mighty Russia, an Orthodox Christian nation like Serbia, announced it would support its brothers in arms. Germany's leader, Kaiser Wilhelm I, was fearful of Serbia's nationalistic ambitions and declared support for Austria-Hungary. Wilhelm had expansionist plans of his own, and a new war was a perfect excuse for him to acquire more land.

Wilhelm wasted little time. On August 2, Germany invaded France, Switzerland, and the little nation of Luxembourg. Just one day later, Germany invaded Russia and officially declared war on France. Then, on August 4, Germany invaded its neighbor to the west, Belgium.

Britain promised it would defend Belgium and entered the war on the side of Serbia, France, and Russia, together known as the Entente Powers. (The United States would not enter the war on the side of the Entente Powers until April 1917.) Germany, Austria-Hungary, and their allies were called the Central Powers. The Croats were struck in the middle but sided with the Central Powers against the Serbs.

Serbia, despite its smaller size, was able to withstand invasions from Austro-Hungarian armies early in the war. Late in 1914 the Serbs formally announced a plan to unite all the South Slavs—the Serbs, Croats, and Slovenes—as part of one state. The plan had to be postponed, though. In spite of the Serbs' initial powerful defense of their land, the inevitable finally happened in late 1915 as Austria-Hungary and its German allies successfully invaded and occupied Serbia. Many Serbian forces were evacuated to the Greek island of Corfu.

The Corfu Declaration

It was on Corfu that concrete steps were taken to make the dream of a unified south Slavic republic reach fruition when representatives of Croatia, Serbia, and the smaller nations of Slovenia and Montenegro took part in a major conference. The main negotiators were an exiled Croatian leader named Ante Trumbić 1864–1938) and the Serbian prime minister

Nikola Pašić (1845–1926). On July 20, 1917, Trumbić and Pašić announced they had come to an agreement, which would be known as the Corfu Declaration.

There were three main points to the pact: (1) The new country would be a parliamentary monarchy under Serb leadership; (2) There would be local autonomy for specific ethnic groups based on social and economic conditions, and the specifics would be worked out at a later date; and (3) A national assembly would meet and adopt a constitution with terms agreed to by a majority. Now they had to wait for the war to end.

Anticipating the conclusion of World War I, United States president Woodrow Wilson (1856–1924) presented to the public on January 8, 1918, his Fourteen Points, guidelines for a peace treaty to take effect at the end of the war. Point number 11 specifically concerned Serbia. It stated that Serbia must be evacuated by Austria-Hungary and Germany and that Serbia would be accorded free and secure access to the sea.

Since Croatia was looked down upon by the United States and the other Entente nations for aligning itself with Austria-Hungary, Trumbić and the Croats knew they had little clout. In September 1918, the Entente Powers swept Austria-Hungary and Germany out of Serbia, and it was obvious that the end of the war was close at hand. A peace treaty was signed on November 11, 1918, at Versailles, near Paris, France.

Decisions by the Balkan peoples regarding unification would have to be made soon. On November 26, Vojvodina, an autonomous district of northern Serbia along the Hungarian border, joined Montenegro in announcing it would join the south Slavic union. While the Croats were gun-shy about joining up with a powerful Serbia, they agreed it was the smartest thing to do in their situation. There was indeed potential for growth and prosperity to be gained from joining forces with the wealthier and more cosmopolitan Serbia.

Kingdom of Serbs, Croats, and Slovenes

On December 1, 1918, Serb crown prince Alexander (1888–1934) proclaimed the new Kingdom of Serbs, Croats, and Slovenes. The capital of the kingdom was Belgrade, also the capital of Serbia.

Yet differences between the many ethnic groups in the new kingdom made it a disaster waiting to happen. The Croats, under the leadership of the Croatian Peasant Party head Stjepan Radić (1871–1928), bitterly expressed their uneasiness about living in a Serb-dominated nation. On February 11, 1921, Radić, on behalf of the majority of the Croatian delegates in parliament, sent a stern message to Alexander. In it he indicted Alexander and the Serb-led government for unneeded violence against non-Serbs. The statement also denied Alexander the right to rule in Croatia.

King Alexander ruled Yugoslavia from 1918 until his assassination in 1934. (Courtesy Free Library of Philadelphia)

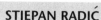

STJEPAN RADIĆ

To Croats everywhere, Stjepan Radić is a true hero. He is viewed by his countrymen as a statesman, a writer, a humanitarian, and a martyr. Radić was born on May 11, 1871, in a village called Trebarjevo, near Sisak in central Croatia. The son of peasants, Radić decided as a young boy that his future was public service. While a high school student, he was often seen taking part in public demonstrations against Hungarian rule. At one demonstration in Zagreb against Hungarian ban Khuen-Héderváry, Radić was jailed and subsequently expelled from high school.

He attended several universities, but his brazen activism constantly got him into trouble. While attending the University of Zagreb, Radić made a public statement against Ban Khuen-Héderváry that led to a four-month jail sentence. While a student at the University of Budapest, Radić burned a Hungarian flag as a protest of a visit by Hungarian king Francis Joseph. He was expelled from the university, sentenced to more time in jail, and banished from all kingdoms and countries represented at the Imperial Council in Vienna.

After release from jail, Radić traveled to Moscow, Russia, then to Paris, France, where he graduated with honors in 1899 from the Free School of Political Science. He was allowed back in Prague, where he was once more arrested for subversive activities and sentenced to time in jail. Finally, Radić returned to Zagreb, where he took an active role in politics, serving as secretary for a coalition of opposition parties.

Some time late in 1904 or early in 1905, Radić and his brother Ante founded the Croatian Peasant Party, a reformist political group. In spite of restrictions on the rights of peasants to vote, the party gradually made headway, earning two seats in the Croatian parliament in

Alexander did just the opposite of what Radić wanted. He called a constitutional convention with the aim of strengthening Serb leadership. Radić and his party protested by boycotting the convention. Instead, on April 1, 1921, the Croatian delegation held their own meeting, approving a Croatian constitution titled "Constitution of the Neutral Peasant Republic of Croatia." The Croats officially declared their own constitution on June 26, 1921.

1908. In 1911, Radić and his wife, Marija, started their own business, the Slavic Bookstore in Zagreb, to earn money to support their family while he rallied for the rights of peasants.

By the end of World War I, Radić was doing very well in his country. His bushy mustache and a salt and pepper beard gave Radić a sophisticated appearance. He campaigned against the union of Croatia and Serbia after the war, concerned about Serb centralism. His party won a majority of 50 seats in parliament in 1920, then won 20 more in 1923. After he and his party boycotted the 1921 constitutional parliament, Radić, flush with the power of the Croatian people behind him, went on a European tour in 1923, visiting Moscow, Paris, and London looking for aid for his cause.

He failed in that regard. Concerned for his safety, he returned to Zagreb, where he lived incognito. In 1925, he was found out and served a short jail sentence, convicted on antigovernment charges stemming from his association with communists while in Moscow.

After his release, Radić changed his strategy and decided to work within the system. He and his associates recognized the constitution, worked peacefully with the Serb opposition while continuing to campaign against what he considered Serb oppression and injustice toward Croats, and served as his nation's minister of education.

Radić resigned his post in 1926, preferring to bring about change through boycotts and other forms of civil disobedience. On June 20, 1928, while engaged in a heated debate in parliament in the kingdom capital of Belgrade, Radić and four other Croatians were shot by a politician named Puniša Radić, a member of the Radical Party, popular in Serbia. Two men died immediately, and three were wounded, including Stjepan Radić. Radić returned to Zagreb, where he died from his wounds on August 8, 1928.

Regardless, Croatia was still legally part of the Kingdom of Serbs, Croats, and Slovenes and without Croatian opposition present at Alexander's constitutional convention, the new constitution he sponsored cruised to an easy victory. It provided for a constitutional monarchy but at the same time adopted a centralized Serbian leadership in the kingdom.

There was symbolic significance for the new constitution. It was declared on June 28, 1921, the anniversary of the Battle of Kosovo Polje

THE USTAŠA

The name *Ustaša* comes from the Croat word *ustanak,* or "insurrection." The Ustaša was founded by Croatian lawyer Ante Pavelić some time between 1926 and 1930, depending on the source, when Pavelić was in exile in Italy. The Ustaša advocated full independence for Croatia and worked underground, in an outright but covert battle against the Serb government.

Pavelić based his group on the nascent Fascist government of Italy being led by Benito Mussolini (1883–1945). Like the Italian Fascist government, the Ustaša glorified the farmer as the backbone of the Croatian people, the family as the central unit, and the Catholic Church as the sacred authority. With its emphasis on freedom from what it considered the oppressive thumb of the Serbian monarchy, the Ustaša immediately drew admiration and support from a wide range of the Croatian people, from students to the clergy.

To the Serbs, the Ustaša was little more than a band of terrorists. It made international news when in 1934 it teamed with a similar group of Macedonians, the VMRO (Internal Macedonian Revolutionary Organization) and assassinated King Alexander while he was in Marseille, France. According to most historians, Pavelić had a direct hand in organizing the murder.

It was not long afterward that the Ustaša evolved from a radical group advocating the political sovereignty of Croatia to an organization propelled by racial superiority. In 1936, Pavelić wrote a text called *The Croat Question* in which he laid out the Ustaša's motivations and goals. Some passages expressed strong nationalism. The text reads in part, "The Croats, a people conscious of their thousand-year-old national individuality, cannot and will not ever give up this individuality, and will resist unconditionally, with all available means, its destruction. The Croat life force is a fact which cannot by affected by any reasons, explanations or arguments, a fact which is indisputable and not subject to discussion. Thus life itself demonstrates the falsehood of the arguments of the victors of the [First] World War. . . ."

However, similarities with the Nazi ideology in Germany were all too obvious in the text, including a strong anti-Semitism. Another segment of Pavelić's text reads as follows: "Today, practically all finance and nearly all commerce in Croatia is in Jewish hands. This became possible only through the support of the state, which thereby seeks, on one hand, to strengthen the pro-Serbian Jews, and on the other, to weaken Croat national strength. . . . In fact, as the Jews had foreseen, Yugoslavia became, in consequence of the corruption of official life in Serbia, a true Eldorado (sic) of Jewry." The Ustaša's hatred of the Jews rivaled its hatred of the Serbs.

In exchange for protection by Italy, the Ustaša furthered Mussolini's policies in the Balkans and the Middle East. Although the Ustaša had made contact with Nazi Germany, the Nazis disassociated themselves from the Ustaša until they invaded Yugoslavia.

After the Nazi invasion of Yugoslavia in 1941, the Ustaša became Hitler's killing force in that corner of the Balkans. In their four years in power, the Ustaša murdered 500,000 Serbs, nearly all the Jews of Croatia, 20,000 Roma (Gypsies), and thousands of political opponents. After the war, Pavelić fled first to Austria, then to Italy, and then Argentina, where he lived openly and worked as head of security for Argentine dictator Juan Perón (1895–1974). After an attempt on his life in the Argentine capital of Buenos Aires, Pavelić escaped to Spain, where he started a new Ustaša cell.

Although Pavelić died on December 28, 1959, in a Madrid hospital, the new Ustaša thrived and was responsible for numerous terrorist attacks in Yugoslavia and elsewhere over the next three decades, among them the murder of four Yugoslavian officials from the 1960s into the early 1970s, numerous hijackings of airplanes, including one of an American airliner in 1976, and the bombing of the Statue of Liberty in 1980; no persons were injured in that blast. In 1986, after four decades of pressure, one of Pavelić's lieutenants during World War II, Andrija Artuković, was deported from the United States. With Croatian independence in the 1990s, the Ustaša's influence has dissipated.

in 1389, in which the Ottoman Empire had defeated Serbia. Since it was passed on St. Vitus's Day, known among the Serbs as Vidovdan, it was named the Vidovdan Constitution.

After serving the jail sentence in 1925, Radić recognized the Vidovdan Constitution and accepted the post of minister of education. In 1928, he and four of his associates were shot in parliament (see sidebar).

After the massacre in Belgrade, the Croatian representatives angrily walked out of parliament. Chaos reigned in Belgrade as protesters of all stripes took to the streets. Radić's successor as leader of the Croatian

Peasant Party, Vlado Maček (1879–1964), was tried for terrorism and sentenced to prison.

With the kingdom seemingly disintegrating before him, Alexander took a bold step and abolished the constitution. He also did away with the legislature, local government, and most civil liberties. Declaring himself absolute ruler, Alexander gave his country a new name, Yugoslavia, or "land of the South Slavs."

As a virtual dictator, Alexander rearranged the nature of his kingdom. No longer would it be divided into the traditional provinces of Croatia, Serbia, and Bosnia and Herzegovina. As an attempt to stop unrest due to ethnic and religious differences, Alexander reorganized the kingdom into new provinces called *banovinas*, each led by a ban, the same title used by medieval rulers in this region.

Unrest continued even after King Alexander relinquished some of his absolute power in 1931. On September 3, he declared that the kingdom would once more have a constitution and legal political parties, although those based on ethnic background or religion would continue to be outlawed. With the Great Depression blanketing the world's economies in the early 1930s, people were unhappy. As a response to the lack of work, poor economic conditions, and Serb domination, some Croats became involved in a small separatist group called Ustaša, led by a Croat national named Ante Pavelić (1889–1959). Members of the Ustaša and Macedonian national extremists murdered Alexander in 1934.

Following the assassination of Alexander, a three-man regency council led by the king's cousin Prince Pavle (1893–1976) took over the reins of government. Alexander's son Peter was officially next in line to become king, but at the time of Alexander's death, he was only 11 years old, too young to rule.

Pavle and his coleaders made a concerted effort to bring more democracy to Yugoslavians, and Croats were pleased when he permitted Croatian Peasant Party leader Vlado Maček to be released from prison. However, Pavle appointed a succession of two prime ministers who courted favor from Mussolini's Fascist Italy and Adolf Hitler's Nazi Germany. The first was a Serb named Milan Stojadinović (1888-1961), who served from June 1935 to February 1939, followed by Dragiša Cvetković (1893–1969). Germany had made major investments in Yugoslavian

industry during the years of the Great Depression, and both prime ministers became friendly with Hitler to court economic favor.

World War II

Beginning in November 1940, Germany ran uncontrolled over eastern
Europe, conquering Hungary, Romania, and Bulgaria in rapid succession.
The world knew Germany had its sights set next on Yugoslavia. Then on
March 27, 1941, the Yugoslav military overthrew Cvetković and named
17-year-old Peter II, Alexander's son, as ruler. Nearly all ethnic and political groups in Yugoslavia, including most Croats, welcomed the change,
knowing that Peter would not ally himself with Hitler.

Just a week and a half later, on April 6, Peter awoke to the chaos of a
Nazi attack on Belgrade. The German air force, the Luftwaffe, led the

*Under the fascist Ustaša, Croatia allied itself with Adolf Hitler's Nazi Germany
during World War II. Here Hitler is seen greeting Croatian prime minister Nikola
Mandić (center) and Foreign Minister Božidar Purić (right).* (Courtesy Library of
Congress)

attack by bombing the Yugoslav capital. A few days later, the Nazis commenced a ground invasion, entering Yugoslavia from land they had captured in Romania and Bulgaria. The new king and his staff were rushed to London in an escape, and Yugoslavia surrendered on April 17.

The Nazis immediately placed Ustaša leader Ante Pavelić in power over a portion of Yugoslavia they called the Independent State of Croatia. Comprised of both Croatia and Bosnia and Herzegovina, it was anything but independent. Pavelić was a puppet, and Hitler pulled his strings, telling him how to run the state. It was then that Pavelić and the Ustaša's killing machine began operation. Serbs who were not killed were forced to convert to Catholicism. Jews and Gypsies in Croatia were not given the choice of conversion; they were sent to death camps to be killed.

Those who had the courage formed resistance groups. Serbs who called themselves Četniks, or Chetniks (both pronounced "Tchetnick"), after the name of Serb warriors from centuries earlier, fought the Ustaša as the official representatives of Peter's government in exile. Some were as brutal as the Ustaša itself.

Also fighting the Ustaša were the Partisans, a group of communists who existed even though the Communist Party was illegal. The leader of the Partisans was a charismatic middle-aged man and long-time activist named Josip Broz (1892–1980).

Broz was a native Croatian, born into a family of 15 children in the village of Kumrovec near the Slovenian border. While in his 20s, he fought in World War I with Austria-Hungary against the Russians. After being captured, he escaped from a Russian prison and took part in the Russian Revolution, fighting with the Communists against Czar Nicholas. After returning home in 1920, he helped organize a metal workers union before joining the Yugoslav Communist Party. Broz was arrested for being a member of a prohibited party and sent to prison. After his release in 1934, Broz took a code name: Tito. In time Tito became Broz's legal last name.

Early in the war, the anticommunist Četniks changed their allegiances, joining the German and Italian fascists against the Partisans. To the Četniks, the fascists were the lesser of two evils. That left Tito's Partisans as the only cohesive force fighting the Nazis, and as a result they began garnering support even from those who had previously been anticommunist. In effect, the Partisans were fighting on two fronts. On the one hand they were battling to get the Nazis out of their land. On the other hand, they were fighting the Četniks for control of Yugoslavia. In November 1942, the Partisans held a conference in the Bosnian town of Bihać. Calling itself the Antifascist Council for the National Liberation of Yugoslavia (AVNOJ, in Serbo-Croatian), they declared their support for equal rights for all and a free enterprise economy.

Italy surrendered in 1943, and the Partisans filled the vacuum left by the retreating Italians. Tito called for a second AVNOJ forum in November 1943 in another Bosnian city, Jajce. Its purpose was to make plans for Yugoslavian leadership following the end of the war.

The Partisans decided to make Tito the marshal and prime minister of Yugoslavia. The exiled King Peter's fate would be decided by a vote. By early 1944 the Allied powers consisting mainly of the United States, Russia, England, and France officially proclaimed they were supporting the Partisans as the chief anti-Nazi force in Yugoslavia. With the help of the Allies, especially the Russians' Red Army, the Partisans emerged victorious in Yugoslavia. Belgrade was liberated from Nazi occupation late in 1944, and Sarajevo in April 1945. The Germans and Ustaša surrendered on May 15, 1945, and the war in Europe was over.

Living Under Tito

Since the Soviet Union was instrumental in relieving the eastern European nations from Nazi occupation, Soviet troops were occupying those nations when Germany surrendered. Soviet dictator Joseph Stalin (1879–1953) had promised the Allies there would be free and open elections in these countries after the war's end, but he did not keep his promise. These countries—Poland, East Germany (Germany had been divided into two separate nations), Hungary, Czechoslovakia, Bulgaria, Romania, and Albania—became satellite states of the Soviet Union. While each had its own leader, they were all under Soviet domination.

However, Tito took over the reins of leadership in Yugoslavia after the war was over. He broke with Stalin in 1948, an anomaly in the region.

For one to understand Tito's form of leadership, which became known as Titoism, it must be stressed that there are different forms of communism.

In pure communism, all business is owned by the community. In the Soviet Union and its bloc of eastern European allies, all business was owned by the government. Citizens could not openly criticize their government under penalty of law. Activists who did were sentenced to prison terms. Religious worship was downplayed, and in some places it was banned outright.

Tito's Yugoslavia was a dictatorship, but a less unyielding one. The elections in Yugoslavia for national assembly leaders in 1945 gave the people no choice; all the candidates were Communists. While Tito did his best to industrialize Yugoslavia following the wreckage wrought by the war, all factories were owned by the federal government, but Tito parted from other European Communist leaders by not having collective ownership of land. People owned the land they worked, and laborers at factories were permitted to form workers' councils. In a system called socialist self-management, these workers' councils were allowed input in their employers' business policies.

While Tito did much to modernize Yugoslavia, many peasants continued to live as they had for centuries. In this 1955 photograph, a farmer plows his fields while his wife leads a team of oxen. (Courtesy United Nations)

A new constitution for Yugoslavia was formulated and affirmed on January 31, 1946. It recognized five distinct nationalities within its borders: the Croats, the Slovenes, the Serbs, the Macedonians, and the Montenegrins. Bosnia's Muslims were initially classified as a religious group with no national identity. In 1968, they were officially recognized as a distinct nationality. In addition, six Yugoslav republics were also recognized: Croatia, Slovenia, Serbia, Bosnia and Herzegovina, Macedonia, and Montenegro. Two Serbian areas, Vojvodina in the north and Kosovo in the south, were declared to be autonomous, or under limited self-rule. However, the republics had little real power. The overwhelming majority of power came out of the nation's capital, Belgrade.

The first 15 years under Tito were relatively benign. Industry expanded, forming the base for a growing economy, but by 1961 the national economy started sputtering in most republics. Croatia proved to be, with Slovenia, the most developed and productive republics in Yugoslavia. In the mid-1960s, Croatia's exports, tourist industry, and migrant workers accounted for more than 40 percent of all of Yugoslavia's foreign-currency earnings.

Some, such as Vladimir Bakarić, the most senior level Croat in Yugoslavia other than of Tito, advocated a severe overhaul of the nation's economy. He encouraged self-management and less centralization in the federal capital in Belgrade. However, Aleksandar Ranković, organizational secretary of the League of Communists (LCY), the official state party, and head of Yugoslavia's secret police, used his clout to steer the nation away from reform and toward continued economic doldrums.

It was only after Tito terminated Ranković for abusing his power, including bugging the phones of other LCY members, that he began to seriously consider economic reform. Tito also led Yugoslavia in expanding trade with the European Economic Community.

By the 1960s, civil unrest was beginning to take seed. One ethnic group after another began to feel it was not getting its fair share from the government. In June 1968, antigovernment riots broke out on the campus of the Workers' University of New Belgrade. Five months later, ethnic Albanians living in Kosovo took to the streets in violent protest. As a result, their grievances were addressed, and they were afforded more representative power. The next year residents of Slovenia rioted after learning that money given by the International Bank of Yugoslavia and allocated toward highway building in their republic had been diverted to road construction projects in Croatia and Serbia.

Croatia was not excluded from the spirit of reform. Early in 1969, young Croats began to show more and more public pride in their ethnicity, expressing their views through rock music and more open media. The heads of the Croatian League of Communists (LCY) were a young woman named Savka Dabčević-Kučar and a young man named Miko Tripalo. To the dismay of national LCY leaders, they embraced the idea of permitting people from noncommunist organizations to take part in discussions regarding economic and political reforms.

This spirit of reform lasted into 1970, when serious discussions began regarding changing the Yugoslav constitution. Tripalo recalled, "Ordinary people were simply no longer prepared to sit and listen to the wise words and advice of the leadership—they wanted to take part themselves in some way, just as the programme of the League of Communists claimed they could."

This spirit of reform was known by several names. One was Maspok, or "mass movement." However, today it is known mainly as the Croatian Spring, and there were times it extended beyond open meetings to street demonstrations. Tito may have favored some minor economic changes, but the participants of the Croatian Spring were advocating radical reforms. It was not just Tito who felt threatened by it. Croatia's own military leaders and hard line communists were scared, too. They convinced Tito that the movement led by Dabčević-Kučar and Tripalo was spinning out of control. Tito used the police and military to crack down on the protestors, and the spirit of liberalism known as the Croatian Spring was wiped out in the cold December of 1971.

Not long afterward, Tito toppled reformist leaders in the republics of Slovenia, Serbia, and Macedonia as well as the Serbian autonomous region of Vojvodina. To stem any more uprisings like the Croatian Spring, Tito's supporters elected him president for life in 1974.

That turned out to be a total of six years. Tito was in his 80s and knew he did not have long to live. He began to consider how the government should be run after he died. There would be no president for life. There would instead be a system of eight rotating presidents, including representatives from each of Yugoslavia's six republics and two autonomous provinces, Vojvodina and Kosovo. Tito hoped that this unusual system of

President Tito made many trips to the United States. Here he visits with former first lady and diplomat Eleanor Roosevelt at her home in Hyde Park, New York, on October 1, 1960. (Courtesy Franklin D. Roosevelt Library)

government would keep the nation unified, since with all ethnic and religious groups represented, none would be able to claim that the government was discriminating against it.

Amid a souring Yugoslavian economy that consisted of a massive foreign debt and beleaguered industry, Tito died on May 4, 1980. His last years in office were not effective ones, but he was eulogized nonetheless as both a national hero and a respected international statesman. The leaders of 49 nations attended his funeral.

The question the world was asking in the spring of 1980 was what would happen to Yugoslavia without the man who had led it for 35 years. The answer was changes on a titanic level that few could have dreamed of in May 1980.

NOTES

p. 26 "'The Croats, a people conscious of their . . .'" Prof. Hugh Agnew, Department of History, George Washington University. "Ante Pavelic: Excerpts from *The Croat Question* (1936)," George Mason University website. Available on-line URL: http://chnm.gmu.edu/history/faculty/kelly/Archive/Yugo/pavelic.htm. Downloaded on January 16, 2003.

pp. 26–27 "'Today, practically all finance and nearly all commerce . . .'" Agnew.

p. 27 "the Ustaša's hatred of the Jews . . ." Simon Wiesenthal Center. "Croatian Terrorist Organization," Simon Wiesenthal Center website. Available on-line. URL: http://motlc.wiesenthal.org/text/x33/xr3345.html. Downloaded on January 16, 2003.

p. 27 "In their four years in power, the Ustaša . . ." Simon Wiesenthal Center website.

p. 33 "In the mid-1960s, Croatia's exports . . ." Misha Glenny, *The Balkans: Nationalism, War and the Great Powers, 1804–1999* (New York: Viking Penguin, 2000), p. 581.

p. 34 "'Ordinary people were simply no longer prepared . . .'" Glenny, p. 591.

3

THE END OF YUGOSLAVIA, CIVIL WAR, AND INDEPENDENCE

The new presidential system took hold, and amid concerns about how the Federal Republic of Yugoslavia (FRY) would manage without the father figure, Tito, at the helm, people tried to go about their daily routines. It was not easy.

The economic situation in the early 1980s in Yugoslavia was dismal. Years of living under communism had made the Yugoslav economy moribund. Another problem was that because of recession that blanketed western Europe in the 1970s, hundreds of thousands of Yugoslav guest workers who had taken jobs in western Europe returned home. The unemployment level in the poorer areas, Macedonia, Bosnia and Herzegovina, and southern Serbia and Kosovo, stood at roughly 20 percent. To create jobs the government found itself continually borrowing money from other nations, leading to a massive increase in Yugoslavia's national debt. In 1982, it was an enormous $18.5 billion. The government had to keep borrowing money just to pay the interest payments.

The federal government decided to investigate methods of rectifying the sour economy. In 1981, it ordered a study of the basic Yugoslav system, called the Long-Term Economic Stabilization Program, or more informally, the Krajgher Commission Report. When it was released in

1983, the report blasted Yugoslavia's communist system of economics, with its impersonal government-managed industry. The report suggested that some sort of free market system must be established to stem the continuing economic downturn. Also in the early 1980s the government passed austerity measures including reducing government spending, with an expected end result of lower, or at least controlled, inflation.

Putting a free market economy into effect might have been a wonderful idea, but practically speaking it was a tough sell to the communist leaders of Yugoslavia's many government bureaus. These veteran bureaucrats were entrenched in their positions and, afraid to lose their jobs, did virtually nothing to put the Krajgher Report's suggestions into effect.

Yugoslavia did get a proverbial shot in the arm in 1984 when it hosted the Winter Olympics at Sarajevo, capital of Bosnia and Herzegovina. For two weeks the ancient Balkan city became a household name internationally. People around the world who knew little about this part of Europe saw the wonderful old city and its surrounding mountains televised on a daily basis. A total of 49 nations sent athletes to the games, and they brought in millions of dollars to the cash-starved economy.

After the Olympics ended, however, things in Yugoslavia got even worse than they had been earlier. Industry continued on its downward path, and communist government officials did little to encourage reform; if anything, most went out of their way to block any such efforts.

Corruption

Reform was needed, and this was proven in 1987 by a bizarre incident that started with a warehouse fire. The warehouse belonged to a company called Agrokomerc, based in the Bosnian town of Velika Kladuša. Agrokomerc was thought by Yugoslavs to have been one of the few shining examples of business under Titoism, but as the fire was investigated, workers from the Bosnian Ministry of Internal Affairs discovered that Agrokomerc was operating on more than $800 million of unsecured loans and did not have hard cash on hand to pay its workers. It was learned that 63 banks had their hands in these financial misdeeds. One Bosnian bank closed right away, and thousands of workers could not cash their paychecks. It was soon revealed that members of the Bosnian government were deeply involved in the Agrokomerc scandal.

As the scandal was further investigated, it became clear that the Agrokomerc incident was not an isolated one. Similar shady dealings were discovered throughout the Yugoslav republics, and in time about 200 Communist Party members in both Bosnia and Croatia were dismissed from their jobs.

By the time the 1980s were coming to an end, it was clear that Tito's system of self-management had failed, and the chief culprit was corruption. Banks, government officials, and business leaders did as much as they could to keep the communist party in control of Yugoslavian industry. For the most part, workplace managers throughout the country did what highly ranked communist party officials told them to do, ignoring input from workers' councils. Their reason for turning a deaf ear to the complaints and advice of their own workers was simple: money. Business managers frequently took bribes from political leaders to keep the status quo, and political leaders took bribes from businessmen and women to look the other way when it came to shoddy and dishonorable business practices.

Meanwhile, by the late 1980s Tito's system of rotating presidents had some unintentional results. While it may have initially reduced the dominance of any particular group in Yugoslavia, by its very nature this method of governing weakened the power of the federal presidency. It loosened the tight rein Tito had once held on the distinct and different republics. This became clear when on September 24, 1986, a newspaper in Belgrade printed a memorandum written by anonymous members of the Serbian Academy of Sciences and Arts (SANU) espousing Serbian nationalism.

The gist of the document was that Serbs living in the autonomous district of Kosovo faced annihilation at the hands of rebellious Albanians, while Serbs in Croatia faced a danger to their lives that they had not encountered since the days of the Ustaša in World War II. It concluded by saying that Serbia's national status must be a top priority.

Communist officials, concerned about keeping a strong federal Yugoslavia, strongly condemned the report, with one exception: The president of the Serbian League of Communists, Slobodan Milošević, criticized the report but kept his remarks private, spoken only at a meeting of the secret police leadership.

Croats followed Serbia's lead, and a movement toward Croatian nationalism began in 1988, when its leadership rebelled against the sectoral government by ending controls on the media and consenting to

FRANJO TUDJMAN

The man who became synonymous with Croatia, Franjo Tudjman, was born in the northwestern Croatian community of Veliko Trgovišće on May 14, 1922. He attended elementary school in his hometown, then moved to Zagreb, where he went to secondary school. During his last years of secondary school, World War II was raging, and Tudjman became an active member of the Partisans. He became known to the Nazis as a dangerous member of the underground. The Nazis feared Tudjman to the extent that they offered money to anyone who would kill him. The Nazis did, in fact, kill his brother in 1943.

Following the war, Tudjman attended the advanced military academy in Belgrade and through his keen military instincts earned the distinction of being appointed the youngest general in Yugoslavia in 1960. Tudjman left the military in 1961 to form his own organization, the Institute for the History of the Labor Movement in Croatia, which was closely tied to the Central Committee of the League of Communists. At the same time, he served on the faculty of the University of Zagreb, where he taught history. A loyal and respected member of the Communist Party, Tudjman earned his doctorate from the university in 1965, specializing in Yugoslavia's history during the royalist period from 1918 to 1941.

That same year, he was elected to parliament, and he simultaneously served as editor of the *Yugoslav Military Encyclopedia* and as a staff member on several other publications. It was also about that time that Tudjman challenged the secret police.

Yugoslavia's secret police chief, Aleksandar Ranković, was put in charge of a commemoration of the 25th anniversary of World War II, emphasizing the victory of the communists over the Nazis. Part of the plans included dedicating a memorial to Yugoslavs who died at the Jasenovac concentration camp. Ranković publicly announced that the total number of victims was between 700,000 and 900,000. Tudjman differed with those figures. Based on research done by his own Institute for the History of the Labor Movement in Croatia, Tudjman felt multiparty elections. A publisher, former army general, and activist named Franjo Tudjman (1922–99) challenged the Communist party by forming a party called the Croatian Democratic Union (HDZ in his

Ranković was exaggerating the number of victims and thought the true figures should be made public. Communist Party officials demanded that Tudjman not release the figures so as not to embarrass either Ranković or the Communist leadership. However, Tudjman assigned one of his associates, Bruno Bušic, to publicly announce the figures. As punishment, Bušic was exiled by the Tito government and hunted down, then murdered by the Yugoslav Secret Police in 1978.

Tudjman was fired as head of the Institute for the History of the Labor Movement in Croatia. Within two years he had been removed from all public government posts, and in 1969 lost his seat in parliament. Tudjman took an active role in the Croatian Spring democracy movement of 1969–71, and for his efforts was convicted in 1972 of counterrevolutionary activity and committing hostile activity against the government. He served nine months in prison and was for a few years stripped of his civil rights, including the rights to speak in public, publish, and travel outside Yugoslavia.

Tudjman courageously bucked the Tito government by speaking with a Swedish reporter in 1977. In the interview he spoke candidly about his views of Yugoslav history, and he openly advocated pluralist democracy. As a result, he was again tried for antigovernment activity and in 1981 was sentenced to three years in prison. Again, he had his civil rights denied, this time for eight years. Tudjman was first imprisoned from January 1982 to February 1983, when he was released after suffering a heart attack. After receiving medical treatment Tudjman was once more sent to prison, in May 1984. Because of his worsening medical condition, he was permanently released in September 1984.

In 1987, Tudjman was allowed to obtain a passport for the first time in 17 years. He took advantage of that freedom by traveling to the United States, Canada, and western Europe, where he spoke to Croatian immigrants and was treated as a prodemocracy hero. In 1989, he founded the Croatian Democratic Union (HDZ), and in 1990 he was elected president of the Republic of Croatia, a post he held until his death in December 1999.

native language). Tudjman took the opposite view of the Serb nationalists, complaining about Serb domination in the Yugoslav government and advocating the formation of a Greater Croatia, which would include the parts of neighboring Bosnia and Herzegovina that had a majority Croat population.

The economy continued its downturn. Frustrated employees went on strike against the management of many Yugoslav businesses. Striking was unheard of during Tito's first couple of decades in power. However, in 1989 alone, an estimated 1,900 strikes occurred.

In the late 1980, residents of all Communist-governed European countries protested in the streets of major eastern European cities, demanding freedom. The civil unrest was in response to a corrupt and tired economic system.

Then, as the decade of the 1980s was winding down, the Berlin Wall, a symbol of communist oppression, came down. Back in 1961 communist East Germany had built the wall in the divided city of Berlin to keep East Germans from escaping into democratic West Berlin. Since then United States presidents from John F. Kennedy to Ronald Reagan publicly called for East Germany to take down the wall.

The East German government never did so, but the citizens of East Germany did. On November 9, 1989, television viewers throughout the world watched live images from Berlin as East Germans took hammers, axes, and other tools and literally smashed the wall to pieces. East German police could not control the crowd; they could only watch as jubilant East Germans cheered and danced while the wall crumbled. People who had witnessed the construction of the wall in 1961 had wondered if it would ever come down in their lifetimes. That day had finally arrived.

After that defining moment, Communist governments in Eastern Europe tumbled like tenpins. On November 10, 1989, the Communist leader of Bulgaria resigned under pressure. On November 28, West German Chancellor Helmut Kohl announced a plan for reunifying Germany as one nation. On December 5, noncommunists took over the majority of the cabinet of another Eastern bloc country, Czechoslovakia. On Christmas Day, perhaps the most oppressive of all the eastern European leaders, Nicolae Ceausescu of Romania, was overthrown and executed by rebellious Romanians. As the 1990s began, there was a new world order.

The End of Yugoslavia

Communist rule was toppled in Yugoslavia, too, but in a less dramatic manner than in the other Eastern bloc countries. It had much to do with burgeoning nationalism, especially in Serbia and Croatia.

Serbia's Milošević, who had taken over as president of the republic in 1989, pushed through a change in Serbia's constitution permitting the annexation of the autonomous districts of Vojvodina and Kosovo, thereby doing away with their own local governments. By taking control of Vojvodina and Kosovo, Milošević blatantly defied the federal Communist leadership of Yugoslavia.

Meanwhile, in 1990 Croatia held general elections in which the anti-communist HDZ (Croatian Democratic Union) did shockingly well against the stalwart League of Communists of Croatia (LCC), taking the majority of seats in the legislature, or Sabor. Tudjman was elected president of Croatia. He tried to calm the nerves of anxious Serbs concerned about his nationalistic tendencies by appointing a Croatian Serb to the post of vice president. It did little good, though. Serbs living near the border of Bosnia and Herzegovina, where memories of Ustaša genocide were still vivid and where Serbs constituted the majority ethnic group, held a referendum in which they proposed autonomy for themselves.

By December 1990, Serbs living in Serb-dominated areas issued declarations of autonomy, and by the following October three Serbian Autonomous Regions (SARs) had been established in Croatia. These were: Krajina, headquartered in Knin; Eastern Slavonia, Baranja, and Western Srem, first headquartered in Dalj, then in Vukovar, in far eastern Croatia; and Western Slavonia. The SARs were not recognized by Croatia, but that did not stop them from declaring themselves the separate Republic of Serbian Krajina (RSK) in December 1990.

Although the central communist party of Yugoslavia was determined to keep Yugoslavia a united nation, it was failing miserably. In December 1990, Croatia's Sabor adopted a new constitution, allowing itself a right to secede from the federal republic as well as authority over its own armed forces. The following March, the Sabor determined that its own legislation would preempt federal legislation. In April, Croatia formed its own national guard, and on May 19, a referendum was held in which 94 percent of the voters said they preferred that Croatia become a sovereign entity, although they left open the option that it remain part of a Yugoslavian confederacy. Most Croatian Serbs boycotted the referendum.

Just over a month later, on June 25, Croatia officially declared its independence from Yugoslavia. That, in effect was the trigger point that started a civil war. The republic of Slovenia also declared its independence, but with Croatia's substantial Serb population, Belgrade was not ready to give up without a fight. The Yugoslav People's Army (JNA) joined with Serbian troops to secure the Serb sections of Slavonia, and by November they controlled a third of Croatia. They also attacked and held the beautiful coastal city of Dubrovnik in October.

Meanwhile, Tudjman appointed members of his government in August, 1991. The vast majority were members of his own HDZ; no members of the Croatian Serb–dominated Serbian Democratic Party were included.

In September, the United Nations (UN) put in place an embargo on arms shipments to the former Yugoslavia. Although periodic cease-fires

The carnage of the Croatian civil war is graphically seen as Serb troops and civilians walk past a dead body and destroyed buildings in November 1991. (AP/Wide World Photos/Srdjan)

were called, fighting continued throughout the fall. Finally, in December the UN decided to send observers to Yugoslavia with the intent of possibly sending peace keeping forces some time in the future. It was on December 23, 1991, that the first European nation, Germany, recognized Croatia. Over the course of early 1992, the other European Community members also recognized Croatia.

Even though Croatia was not yet a member of the UN, the world body tried arranging another cease-fire. At the end of 1991, civil war casualties had totaled over 6,000 dead, 23,000 wounded, and 400,000 internally displaced people in Croatia. Finally, on January 2, 1992, JNA and the Croatian National Guard signed an unconditional cease- fire sponsored by the UN. By the end of February, the UN Protection Force (UNPROFOR) of 14,000 troops arrived in Croatia. It was the largest, most expensive, and most complex peace operation in UN history, but it was a necessary expense in the efforts to find some solutions to the difficulties faced by the people living in the former Yugoslav republics.

UNPROFOR's immediate job was to supervise the withdrawal of the JNA from Croatia and demilitarize the areas held by Serbs. These areas were set aside as United Nations Protected Areas (UNPAs). By mid-May 1992, the JNA began withdrawing from Croatia, and the siege of Dubrovnik came to an end on May 28. It was also in May when Croatia was admitted to the UN.

Civil War Continues

Despite these initial successes, civil war did not end quickly. Serbian troops expelled more than 1,000 non-Serbs from the Eastern Slavonia section of Croatia, and the Croats fought back, shelling Serb-dominated areas. The UN, alert to the situation, intervened and proclaimed a resolution calling for the Croats to withdraw to positions they had held prior to June 21 and to no longer invade Serb-dominated regions. Croatia grudgingly complied.

The first elections under Croatia's new constitution were held on August 2, 1992. Franjo Tudjman was overwhelmingly reelected, and his party, the HDZ, won 85 of the 138 seats in the Chamber of Representatives, the larger of the legislature's two houses. The other house, the

Chamber of Counties, held its elections on February 7, 1993, and the HDZ won 37 of the 63 seats.

In late August 1992, RSK (Republic of Serbian Krajina) leaders announced they were no longer seeking independence. Things seemed to be on a positive road in Yugoslavia. In September Yugoslavian prime minister Milan Panić (1929–   ) declared that his country would recognize an independent Croatia if Croatia stayed within the borders it had had prior to the breakout of civil war in mid-1991. Panić also required that the Serb-dominated areas be given special consideration. Peace talks were held in London in which the RSK and Croatia's leaders reached a pact based on economic cooperation. Tudjman and Federal Republic of Yugoslavia president Dobrica Ćosić also agreed to forge ahead in regards to normalizing relations.

However, from the fall of 1992 on, things stopped proceeding smoothly. Civil war was also raging to Croatia's south, in the former Yugoslav republic of Bosnia and Herzegovina (BiH). There was no dominant ethnic group in BiH, a new nation split between Serbs, Croats, and Muslims known as Bosniaks. A group of Bosnian Croats, headed by Mate Boban (1940–97), wanted to break away from BiH. On October 24, 1992, Boban proclaimed the Bosnian Croats' own Croatian Union of Herzeg-Bosnia. He declared that the ancient Bosnian city of Mostar was its capital that and sole authority was the Croatian National Guard.

Boban's nationalist rebels were fully supported by Franjo Tudjman, who had sent his own troops to aid their fight. That drew the sharp criticism of Great Britain's David, Lord Owen, a cochairman of the peace talks taking place in London. Under the threat of sanctions administered by the European Community, Owen ordered Croatia to pull its troops out of Bosnia. He also leveled the charge of ethnic cleansing against Croatia, accusing Tudjman and his troops of attempting to expel native Bosnians from the Croatian-dominated portion of BiH in order to make it a purely Croatian entity. The concept of ethnic cleansing dominated the news that year, as the international community loudly accused Serbia of the same crime in BiH. Although Tudjman denied the charges, most independent observers believe Croatia was guilty.

Bloodshed was the rule in the former Yugoslavia in 1993. As Croatia and Serbia continued to fight the Bosnians in the BiH, Croatia had its hands full at home. Croatia initiated a battle in the Serb-held area of Krajina over a destroyed bridge they accused the UN of not replacing. Residents of Istria, a peninsula in northwestern Croatia, were demanding autonomy. There was also a huge refugee problem, with tens of thousands of displaced persons from Bosnia and Herzegovina seeking asylum in Croatia.

On November 9, 1993, an incident occurred which came to symbolize the senseless carnage of the war. Croatian soldiers destroyed the centuries-old Mostar Bridge over the Neretva River in the Croatian-dominated city of Mostar in BiH. It was a stately marble structure that had spanned the Neretva since 1566 and had stood through scores of natural disasters. Its destruction fanned the flames of retaliation. If the Croats destroyed a Muslim mosque, Bosnian Muslims attacked a Catholic church. After Muslims killed more than 35 Croat civilians in the town of Križ in September 1993, Croatian soldiers murdered Muslim villagers in Stupni Do in October.

As 1993 became 1994, war continued on all fronts, but Croatia and the Federal Republic of Yugoslavia offered olive branches to each other in January 1994 when they each announced their intentions of opening diplomatic offices in both Zagreb and Belgrade. However, Croatia also made enemies when it threatened to intervene more deeply in BiH to aid Bosnian Croats. United States ambassador to the UN, Madeleine Albright, threatened stiff economic sanctions if Croatia fulfilled that promise. Tudjman publicly changed his mind in March and agreed to the concept of a Bosniak-Croat federation in Bosnia and Herzegovina. Then on March 30 a cease-fire negotiated by Russian diplomats called for a truce between Croatia and the RSK, with UNPROFOR troops assigned to keep the peace.

Peace talks between all the parties involved in the fighting stagnated through the summer. The question of whether there would be autonomy for the Croatian Serbs in Krajina was deadlocked. In October, a new association of peace negotiators, informally called the Zagreb Group, was formed to tackle the sticky question. The Zagreb Group consisted of four people: the United States and Russian ambassadors to Croatia and two representatives from the European Union (EU), formerly the European Community (EC). Both RSK leader Borislav Mikelić and Franjo Tudjman initially took hard line positions with the Zagreb Group. In January 1995, Tudjman went so far as to order UNPROFOR troops out of Croatia, since he claimed their presence only reinforced the Serbs' position.

Criticism from other nations was fierce. On March 12, 1995, two weeks before the UNPROFOR troops were about to leave, Tudjman changed his mind. He said he would allow a smaller force of UN troops on hand. An agreement was reached, and a force called the United Nations Confidence Restoration Operation (UNCRO), consisting of several hundred troops, took positions along Croatia's borders with Bosnia and Herzegovina and the FRY.

Still, even after four years, the fighting did not let up. Stating that they needed to open a blocked highway between Zagreb and Belgrade, Croatian troops invaded the SAR of Western Slavonia on May 1–2, 1995. The highway was opened to civilian traffic the next day, but in response to the attack, Croatian Serbs fought back immediately, killing six civilians in Zagreb. Serb President Milošević publicly condemned the civilian killings. The UN did not delay in their response, and through the international body's efforts, the two sides agreed to a cease-fire under the following conditions: Serb civilians and soldiers in Western Slavonia were allowed safe passage into Bosnia and Herzegovina, but the Serbs had to surrender their weapons to the UN.

Not all Croatian Serbs were united in the support of a separate Serb entity outside Serbia. Proof was offered on May 21, when the RSK Assembly voted on the region's future. The RSK's two most powerful officers took different stands, with President Milan Martić voting to unify Bosnian Serb and Croatian Serb territories, and Prime Minister Borislav Mikelić speaking out against the idea.

Regardless of RSK votes, Croatia had its own agenda, which became clear on August 4, when Croatian troops embarked on a massive invasion into Krajina. After their capture of the Serb-dominated territory, a mass exodus of Croatian Serbs resulted. It is estimated that about 150,000 people escaped or were forced to leave, with most relocating to Serbia or Serb-dominated regions of Bosnia and Herzegovina. After the reacquisition of Krajina, Croatia allowed a few hundred thousand Croat and Muslim Bosnian refugees to relocate there.

In spite of the UN sponsored cease-fire, the fighting in Croatia went unabated. In the fall of 1995 serious skirmishes between Croatian troops and rebel Serbs were reported in Eastern Slavonia. President Tudjman threatened to use his Croatian military to annex Eastern Slavonia. Negotiations brokered by a UN diplomat, Thorvald Stoltenberg, and the U.S. ambassador to Croatia, Peter Galbraith, were held in the Serb-held town of Erdut and resulted in an 11-point agreement. The most important decision was to declare a transitional period in which the UN would administer order in Eastern Slavonia until the region was demilitarized. Then a joint Croat-Serb police force would take over. Another point agreed upon by all sides called for the safe return of refugees.

In the meantime, elections for city officials were held in Zagreb in October 1995. Even though candidates from opposition parties received more votes than Tudjman's ruling party, the HDZ, Tudjman vetoed four opposition candidates for mayor and installed a candidate from his party. He then organized a referendum to redistrict Zagreb, but most of the capital's citizens boycotted it. This local disagreement turned into a stalemate, which continued until 1997, when the HDZ gained control of the

November 3, 1995: A Croatian Serb soldier smokes a cigarette in the frontline village of Tenja in Eastern Slavonia, Croatia, while at the same time, thousands of miles away, peace negotiations were taking place in Dayton, Ohio.
(AP/Wide World Photos/Srdjan)

city council. International human rights group observed Tudjman's attempted control grab with disdain.

Peace at Last

U.S. president Bill Clinton and his staff, including mediator Richard Holbrooke, had been trying for some time to get all warring parties in former Yugoslavia—especially the Bosnians and Serbs—to sit down and work out their problems. In mid-October Holbrooke and other diplomats traveled throughout Europe, including the capitals of all the former Yugoslav republics, urging the parties to talk. All that hard work paid off when peace negotiations began on November 1, 1995, at Wright-Patterson Air Force Base in Dayton, Ohio.

Meanwhile, back in Erdut, representatives from Croatia and Eastern Slavonia signed a treaty on November 12 spelling out the details for the reintegration of Eastern Slavonia into Croatia. The UN-supervised transitional period would last two years, and the UN would oversee the demilitarization and the return of refugees. On January 16, 1996, the UNCRO mandate expired. On that day the UN Security Council established the 5,000-troop United Nations Transitional Administration for Eastern Slavonia, Baranja, and Western Srem (UNTAES) to take over peace keeping duties in the region. An American diplomat named Jacques Paul Klein was put in charge of supervising UNTAES.

The war in Bosnia officially ended on November 21, 1995, when a comprehensive peace treaty between Croatia's Tudjman, Serbia's Milošević and Bosnia and Herzegovenia's leader, Alija Izetbegović was signed in Dayton. In the treaty text, all parties agreed in general to respect each other's sovereign equality, to cooperate fully with the Security Council, to settle disputes by peaceful means, and to grant refugees the right to return home safely and regain any lost property. The treaty was signed in Paris by Tudjman, Milošević, and Izetbegović on December 14, 1995.

In human terms, the four years of war were exorbitantly costly. About 200,000 people had been killed in the fighting, and more than 2 million had been displaced.

Peace at last: Croatia's president, Franjo Tudjman, prepares to sign the peace treaty at Wright-Patterson Air Force Base in Dayton, Ohio, on November 10, 1995. (AP/Wide World Photos/ Al Behrman)

Now that there was peace, the question was whether it would hold. Many, especially in the United States and Europe, feared the worst—that ethnic tensions would be stronger than a treaty and that fighting would break out again, this time with Americans and Europeans dying in battle.

Surprisingly to many, that has not happened. The peace has been uneasy, but it has held.

Postwar Croatia

Now the postwar parties that had fought against each other had the unenviable job of reconstructing their countries. In May 1996, the Croatian Chamber of Representatives passed legislation granting amnesty for any crimes committed during the civil war—with the exception of those considered war crimes—beginning in August 1990. The logic behind the move was to help speed the return of refugees. Around the same time the demilitarization of Eastern Slavonia took place, finishing in 30 days. Then, in November, the UN Security Council, with the intent of keeping the peace, extended the UNTAES agreement to keep the peace-keeping troops on hand for six more months, into July 1997.

The year 1997 was noteworthy in Croatia for both elections and indictments. The first election was a referendum that took place in Eastern Slavonia among Serbian Croats in April. Although both the country of Croatia and the UN called the election illegitimate, the vast majority of voters elected to keep Eastern Slavonia a separate administrative area under Serb control after the territory was returned to Croatia.

Then, on April 13, elections to Croatia's Chamber of Counties were held, with the HDZ emerging as the big winner, taking 42 of the 63 total seats. Elections for president were held on June 15. Although Franjo Tudjman was widely reported to be in poor health, he was overwhelmingly reelected with 61.4 percent of the vote. While some international human rights or political groups observing these elections said that despite some irregularities they were basically fair, others have disagreed and stated that the ruling party was afforded unfair advantages, including restricting the media.

Later that month the first indictments for war crimes were handed out by the United Nations International Criminal Tribunal for the Former Yugoslavia (ICTY). The ICTY was established by the United Nations Security Council on May 25, 1993. Based in The Hague, the de facto capital of The Netherlands, the tribunal has jurisdiction for persons accused of war crimes, crimes against humanity, and genocide in former Yugoslavia occurring since January 1, 1991. Slavko Dokmanović, a Serb who had been mayor of Vukovar, Eastern Slavonia, in the early 1990s, was charged with the deaths of 260 civilians in his city in November 1991. Dokmanović's trial began in January 1998 and lasted until June 28, 1998, but three days following its end, before any verdict could be reached, Dokmanović hanged himself in his jail cell.

The problem of displaced persons was still a major one. Concerned that the return of refugees would further destabilize Eastern Slavonia, in June the UN Security Council resolved to extend the UNTAES mandate for six more months, over the Croatian government's strong objections. Although by mid-December only a few thousand of the estimated 80,000 refugees had returned to Eastern Slavonia, control of the Transitional Police Force in Eastern Slavonia was transferred to Croatia's Ministry of Internal Affairs, and in mid-January, the UNTAES mandate was declared finished. Control of Eastern Slavonia was officially turned over to Croatia.

In much of 1998 Tudjman had his hands full, not just because of the problems associated with bringing life back to normal in Eastern Slavonia. Croats in the nation's capital, Zagreb, took to the streets in February, protesting living conditions that had not greatly improved since the end of the war. Several protestors were injured in confrontations with local authorities. In order to minimize the chances for such violent unrest again, the government in April passed several laws regulating public demonstrations.

Then, in September, a minor financial scandal reported in local media soon threatened to bring down the Tudjman government. Tudjman's wife, Ankica, held a bank account that he had never made public, an act required according to local law. Opposing parties clamored for Tudjman's resignation.

Another scandal broke out concerning, of all things, a beauty pageant. The declared winner of the Miss Croatia contest, a preliminary event before the Miss World competition, Lejla Sehović, had her title taken away by pageant officials citing voting irregularities. The fact that Sehović was Muslim caused doubters to claim religious bias, especially after a Croat woman was chosen Miss Croatia in her stead. Other nations agreed with those claiming discrimination and as a result of world pressure Sehović was permitted to represent Croatia in the 1998 Miss World pageant.

Croatia's farmers were the next group to voice dissatisfaction with their government. They charged that inept government policies were causing them to suffer economically. Under pressure, Croatia's minister of agriculture and forestry was replaced in February 1999.

The once popular President Tudjman was now seen by much of the Croatian populace as the head of a corrupt government who had become a virtual dictator. He allowed himself the final word in governmental matters and held tight control over the Croatian media.

Through all these internal problems, Western nations and the UN kept a close watch on the human rights situation in Croatia and did not like what they saw. In the spring of 1999, the United States publicly criticized Croatia's human rights policies. According to the U.S. report, the Croatian government was not cooperating with the ICTY to its full capacity. It was not expediting the reintegration of Serbian Croat refugees, and it was blocking any effort at a free press in the nation's media, which it controlled.

Citing what he considered his country's continuing erosion of freedoms, Croatia's deputy prime minister, Milan Ramljak (who concurrently was the minister of justice), resigned in protest in April. By late summer, Tudjman had reorganized the government, giving important posts to people who were friendlier toward his viewpoints.

Tudjman and the Croatian leadership wanted to begin legal proceedings against the Federal Republic of Yugoslavia that summer for crimes of genocide committed against Croats during the civil war years. That was fine with the ICTY as long as Croatia cooperated in return. Croatia was willing to extradite one suspected war criminal, Vinko Martinović, wanted for alleged war crimes committed against Muslims in 1993 and 1994. However, Croatia was hesitant to turn over another suspect, Mladen Naletilić, accused of similar crimes. After threats of economic sanctions from the United States, Crotia began to soften its stance and to make efforts to extradite Naletilić in the fall of 1999. Extradition was postponed until after Naletilić's recovery from surgery.

Naletilić was not the only prominent Croatian figure to undergo medical treatment at that time. Just after announcing that elections to Croatia's Chamber of Representatives would take place in December, Franjo Tudjman underwent an emergency operation. His recovery progressed poorly, and on November 26 Tudjman was declared by the Sabor to be temporarily incapacitated or not healthy enough to run the government. The incumbent parliamentary speaker, Vlatko Pavletić, took over the government's reins and rescheduled elections to the Chamber of Representatives for January 3, 2000.

A New President

On December 10, 1999, Tudjman died, and an election for a new president was slated for January 24, 2000. In the elections to the Chamber of Representatives, the HDZ came out the big loser. A coalition of small parties took 71 of the 151 chamber seats, while the once mighty HDZ garnered only 45.

Since none of the several presidential candidates received 50 percent of the vote in the January 24 federal election, a second round of voting between the two front runners took place on February 7. Former FRY president Stipe Mesić, head of the Croatian People's Party, received 56.2 percent of the votes, while runner-up Dražen Budiša took 43.8 percent. Mesić was sworn in as president on February 18, 2000.

The Mesić government has done much to transfer power from the presidency to the parliament. (See chapter 4, Government, for further details.) His moderate approach has been credited by citizens of Croatia and elsewhere for giving his country the political and economic respectability it was lacking under Tudjman. On the foreign affairs front, Mesić ended government support for the ultranationalist Croatians who supported the annexation of Croatian sections of Bosnia and Herzegovina.

Since his election, Mesić has faced a series of ups and downs. At times he has been both credited and condemned concerning Croatia's cooperation with the International Criminal Tribunal for the Former Yugoslavia (ICTY) (see chapter four, government). In July 2001, the Mesić government survived a vote of no confidence brought by nationalists who disagreed with his willingness to cooperate with the ICTY.

A major milestone occurred in April 2002 when Croatia's foreign minister, Tonino Picula, went to Belgrade to meet with the Serbian foreign minister. It was the first such meeting since Croatia became independent. In July, Mesić's prime minister, Ivica Račan, resigned. He felt that political infighting was damaging national economic reform. A new era in Croatian history was under way.

NOTES

p. 37 "The unemployment level in the poorer areas . . ." Glenny, Misha. *The Balkans: Nationalism, War and the Great Powers, 1804–1999* (New York: Viking Penguin, 2000), p. 623.

p. 37 "In 1982, it was an enormous . . ." Glenny. p. 623.

p. 42 "However, in 1989 alone, an estimated . . ." Donia, Robert J., and John V. A. Fine, Jr. *Bosnia and Herzegovina: A Tradition Betrayed* (New York: Columbia University Press, 1994), p. 199.

p. 44 "Most Croatian Serbs boycotted . . ." "Croatia." *The Europa World Yearbook*, Volume 1 (London: Europa Publications, 2000), p. 1,143.

p. 45 "At the end of 1991, civil war casualties . . ." *The Europa World Yearbook*. p. 1,143.

p. 45 "By the end of February . . ." *The Europa World Yearbook.* p. 1,143.

p. 45 "It was the largest, most expensive . . ." Ilic, Igor, and Slavoljob Leko. "UNPROFOR Facts and Figures." Available on-line. URL: http://www.hr. hrvatska/WAR/UNPF-facts.html. Downloaded on September 11, 2002.

p. 47 "After Muslims killed more than . . ." Donia and Fine. p. 256.

p. 48 "It is estimated that about 150,000 . . ." *The Europa World Yearbook.* p. 1,145.

p. 50 "In human terms, the four years . . ." British Broadcasting Corporation. "Bosnian leaders embrace new era." July 15, 2002. Available on-line. URL:http:// news.bbc.co.uk/2/hi/europe/2128641.stm. Downloaded on September 14, 2002.

p. 52 "Then, on April 13, elections . . ." *The Europa World Yearbook.* p. 1,147.

p. 52 "Although Franjo Tudjman . . ." *The Europa World Yearbook.* p. 1,147.

p. 55 "Former FRY president, Stipe Mesić . . ." *The Europa World Yearbook.* p. 1,148.

PART II
Croatia Today

4

GOVERNMENT

No one would expect it to be easy for any nation to make a transformation from a one-party communist government to a parliamentary democracy. A total of four years of civil war plus continuing ethnic strife has further complicated matters in Croatia. Nevertheless, the Croats are holding their own, and the Croatian government is progressing in a more orderly way than many had predicted.

The Original Constitution

Even though Croatia, officially called the Republic of Croatia, did not formally declare its independence until June 25, 1991, it declared and enacted a new constitution in 1990. The designers of the new Croatian constitution spelled out their prime goals in a section of the constitution titled "Basic Provisions."

Article 1 of the section reads in part, "The Republic of Croatia is a unitary and indivisible democratic and social state. Power in the Republic of Croatia derives from the people and belongs to the people as a community of free and equal citizens." According to Article 3, "Freedom, equal rights, national equality and equality of genders, love of peace, social justice, respect for human rights, inviolability of ownership, conservation of nature and the environment, the rule of law, and a democratic multiparty system are the highest values of the constitutional order of the Republic of Croatia and the ground for interpretation of the Constitution."

Specifically, the constitution calls for a government consisting of three branches: executive, legislative, and judicial. The executive branch is led by the president, elected by popular vote for a five-year term. With memories of one-party Communist rule still fresh in the minds of most Croatians in 1990, the constitution declared that the president would be limited to two total terms in office. With the consent of parliament, the president would appoint a prime minister and members of the cabinet.

However, according to the 1990 constitution, the president was given extraordinarily strong powers. He was allowed to appoint and dismiss members of the government and dissolve parliament as he wished. He was also given the right to rule by decree during emergency, including wartimes.

The prime ministerial candidate must be approved by parliament. His responsibilities include working with the cabinet to propose a national budget and any federal laws, as well as plan and guide the nation's foreign policies. Other major government officials include a minister of foreign affairs, a first deputy prime minister, and three additional deputy prime ministers.

The legislative branch, parliament, is the Sabor. According to the 1990 constitution, it was to consist of two bodies, an upper house, the Županski Dom, or Chamber of Counties, and a lower house, the Zastupnički Dom, or Chamber of Representatives. The 127 members of the House of Representatives are elected directly by the people. The framers of the constitution intended the lower house to reflect the entire population of Croatia. With that in mind, they added provisions to the constitution so that if minority communities were not fairly represented, additional members could be added. These included Serbs, Bosniaks, Albanians, Czechs, Hungarians, Slovenes, Montenegrins, and Romas (Gypsies).

One unusual measure in the original constitution was the granting of suffrage in the Republic of Croatia's federal elections to persons of Croatian ethnicity living outside the republic. These people were regarded by the government as Diaspora Croats. Any person 18 years of age or older is entitled to vote, while any employed person 16 years of age or older can legally vote.

The Upper House consisted of 68 members, including three members of each of the 21 counties, all elected directly by the people. The remaining five members were appointed by the president. The intent of these five at-large seats was to ensure that minority voices would be heard in the Sabor.

Terms for members of both houses totaled four years. It was the job of the House of Counties to propose new laws or ask for reconsideration of existing laws, while the House of Representatives was in charge of adopting all laws. General powers of the Sabor include passage of laws, adoption of the nation's budget, setting the nation's political boundaries, carrying out elections and certain appointments to office, and declarations of war and peace. According to the constitution, the Sabor is to meet in two sessions a year, from January 15 to July 15 and from September 15 to December 15.

The Judicial System

Croatia's basic judicial system is similar to the one used in the former Yugoslavia. There are three main tiers: municipal courts, county courts, and the Supreme Court. The Croatian court system is one of trials and appeals. The Supreme Court is the nation's highest court, and its job is to ensure uniform application of the law. Supreme Court judges are appointed by the National Judicial Council, consisting of 11 men or women who are nominated by the Chamber of Counties and elected by the House of Representatives. Judges are appointed for life unless they willingly resign. It is the custom of the republic to keep the Supreme Court's hearings open to the public.

In addition, Croatia has a 13-member Constitutional Court that works to assure that all laws conform to the republic's constitution. The judges belonging to this court are appointed by parliament and serve eight-year terms.

Like most countries right after war, the Republic of Croatia has an active military consisting of an army, a navy, and an air force. Male citizens are obligated to serve in some branch of the military for a period of at least 10 months when they turn 19.

A LONG NATIONHOOD SPELLED OUT IN THE CONSTITUTION

Today's Republic of Croatia has a long and sometimes strange heritage, consisting of both periods of glory and periods of shame. Intriguingly, the founders of the new nation decided to reference their nation's long history in justification of their right to independence in what is essentially the preamble to their constitution. Titled "Historical Foundations," this introduction to the Republic of Croatia follows:

> The millenary identity of the Croatian nation and the continuity of its statehood, confirmed by the course of its entire historical experience within different forms of states and by the preservation and growth of the idea of a national state, founded on the historical right of the Croatian nation to full sovereignty, manifested in:
>
> - the formation of Croatian principalities in the seventh century;
> - the independent mediaeval state of Croatia founded in the ninth century;
> - the Kingdom of Croats established in the tenth century;
> - the preservation of the identity of the Croatian state in the Croatian-Hungarian personal union;
> - the independent and sovereign decision of the Croatian Parliament (Sabor) of 1527 to elect a king from the Habsburg dynasty;
> - the independent and sovereign decision of the Croatian Parliament of the Pragmatic Sanction of 1712;
> - the conclusions of the Croatian Parliament of 1848 regarding the restoration of the Triune Kingdom of Croatia under the authority of the Banus grounded on the historical, national and natural right of the Croatian nation;
> - the Croatian-Hungarian Compromise of 1868 on the relations between the Kingdom of Dalmatia, Croatia and Slavonia and the Kingdom of Hungary, grounded on the legal traditions of both states and the Pragmatic Sanction of 1712;
> - the decision of the Croatian Parliament of 29 October 1918 to dissolve state relations between Croatia and Austria-Hungary and the simultaneous affiliation of independent Croatia, invoking its historical and natural right as a nation, with the state of Slovenes, Croats and Serbs, proclaimed on the former territory of the Habsburg Monarchy;
> - the fact that the Croatian Parliament had never sanctioned the decision of the National Council of the State of Slovenes, Croats

and Serbs to unite with Serbia and Montenegro in the Kingdom of Serbs, Croats and Slovenes (1 December 1918), subsequently (3 October 1929) proclaimed the Kingdom of Yugoslavia;

- the establishment of the Home Rule (Banovina) of Croatia in 1939, by which Croatian state identity was restored within the Kingdom of Yugoslavia,
- establishing the foundations of state sovereignty during the course of the Second World War, by the decisions of the Antifascists Council of National Liberation of Croatia (1943), as opposed to the proclamation of the Independent State of Croatia (1941), and subsequently in the Constitution of the People's Republic of Croatia (1947) and all later constitutions of the Socialist Republic of Croatia (1963–1990), on the threshold of the historical changes, marked by the collapse of the communist system and changes in the European international order, the Croatian nation by its freely expressed will at the first democratic elections (1990) reaffirmed its millenary statehood.

By the new Constitution of the Republic of Croatia (1990) and the victory in the Homeland War (1991–1995), the Croatian nation demonstrated its will and determination to establish and defend the Republic of Croatia as a free, independent, sovereign and democratic state. Considering the presented historical facts and universally accepted principles of the modern world, as well as the inalienable and indivisible, non-transferable and non-exhaustible right of the Croatian nation to self-determination and state sovereignty, including its fully maintained right to secession and association, as basic provisions for peace and stability of the international order, the Republic of Croatia is established as the national state of the Croatian nation and the state of the members of autochthonous national minorities: Serbs, Czechs, Slovaks, Italians, Hungarians, Jews, Germans, Austrians, Ukrainians and Ruthenians and the others who are citizens, and who are guaranteed equality with citizens of Croatian nationality and the realization of national rights in accordance with the democratic norms of the United Nations Organization and the countries of the free world. Respecting the will of the Croatian nation and all citizens, resolutely expressed in the free elections, the Republic of Croatia is hereby founded and shall develop as a sovereign and democratic state in which equality, freedoms and human rights are guaranteed and ensured, and their economic and cultural progress and social welfare promoted.

Changes to the Constitution

After the death of Franjo Tudjman the people of Croatia began to reconsider the strength of the powers the constitution gave to the office of the president. Concerned that the president might have too much leeway, lawmakers drafted a series of amendments in November 2000 that weakened presidential power and gave more final say to the Sabor.

These amendments included: switching general authority over the government from the president to the Sabor, barring the president from political party membership, adding various conditions making it more difficult for the president to dissolve parliament, and abolishing suffrage for Diaspora Croats. In the spring of 2001, perhaps the biggest change in Croatia's government was made when the Sabor abolished the Chamber of Counties. The Sabor is now a unicameral body with just a 151-member Chamber of Representatives.

Political Parties

Croatian citizens have plenty of choices when election day arrives. There exist in the nation today roughly 80 political parties representing all ends of the political spectrum, from the most middle-of-the-road to extremes on both the right and the left.

For most of the young republic's existence the Croatian Democratic Union (HDZ) under Franjo Tudjman was the dominant party. It was founded by Tudjman in 1988, and most observers tended to view it as a distinct but not necessarily extreme nationalist party. Its prime membership consisted of a wide range of Croatian citizens, including devout Catholics, former Communist officials, ardent nationalists, and market reform liberals. The HDZ has in recent years suffered from policy disagreement among its members, with some of its activists concentrating on improving Croatia's domestic economic development and others who believe the party should be more concerned about ethnic Croats living in Bosnia and Herzegovina. Tudjman's death initially left the party in chaos. A huge reorganization was in order, and many hard liners bolted from the party. This included the sitting minister of foreign affairs, Mate Granić, who had his eye on the presidency. He lost, however, to Stipe Mesić.

Following Tudjman's death, the members of five moderate parties got together and formed a coalition, put together as a direct response to what was seen as Tudjman's authoritarian leanings. The coalition helped elect Stipe Mesić, formerly a Tudjman disciple, to the presidency.

Two parties dominated the new coalition. One was the Social Democratic Party (SDP), the other was the Croatian Social Liberal Party (HSLS). The SDP tends to lean a little left of center. It aligns itself with labor unions, women, and ethnic minorities, including Croatian Serbs.

The HSLS, founded in 1989, generally supports positions that are to the right of center. It supports the basic social and liberal economic policies practiced in much of Europe, but with an emphasis on the individual citizen's rights and respect for the role of the state in society. At first the HSLS had a strong nationalistic plank in its platform, although that has all but disappeared.

Another party with a major role in the coalition is the Croatian Peasant Party (HSS), a slightly right of center rural-based organization that is the direct descendent of Stjepan Radić's old Croatian Peasant Party of the 20th century. After all those decades, it has not forgotten its roots. Groups that make up the majority of the party's active members include: the Croatian Peasants' Association (a group of peasants and food manufacturers), the Farming Association (a cooperative of food manufacturers), and Peasants United (an organization devoted to the preservation of traditional values and folk customs).

The remaining two parties that formed the coalition are smaller ones: the Croatian Christian Democratic Union (HKDU) and the Croatian Rights Party (HSP). The HKDU is seen mainly as a conservative Christian democratic party and might be best known for its leader, Marko Veselica, a strong nationalist and anticommunist who spent 11 years in jail as a political criminal during Tito's reign. The HSP was founded at the beginning of the Croatian civil war by Dobroslav Paraga, an ultranationalist, and has not shied away from publically claiming its admiration for the old Ustaša which cooperated with Nazi Germany during World War II. Together, the HKDU and HSP won 5 percent of the vote in the 2000 election.

There are several other active but minority political parties in Croatia. One is the Serbian People's Party (SNS) led by Milan Djukić. Its

STIPE MESIĆ

Croatia's second president, Stipe Mesić, was formally named Stjepan Mesić at birth on December 24, 1934, in the northern Croatian community of Orahovica. The son of a civil servant and homemaker, Mesić attended law school at the University of Zagreb. When not studying he was usually busying himself as an activist for better workers' rights. Mesić graduated law school in 1961 and moved back to his hometown. In 1966 he was elected mayor of Orahovica.

Mesić continued his activism by taking an active role in the Croatian Spring reform movement of 1969–71 and as a result served one year in prison. In the early 1990s he joined Franjo Tudjman's Croatian Democratic Union (HDZ) and served as the HDZ executive committee's secretary, then chairman. In Yugoslavia's first free elections in 1990, Mesić and Tudjman's HDZ came to power and Mesić was appointed the first prime minister of Croatia. The Sabor decided that the man with the short-cropped hair, bushy eyebrows, and salt-and-pepper beard and mustache should be Croatia's member of the Yugoslav presidency. He held the post until Yugoslavia self-destructed and is noteworthy in Balkan history for being the last president of the six-republic nation known as Yugoslavia.

Mesić was elected Speaker of Croatia's parliament in 1992. Around that time he became disenchanted with Tudjman, especially his ideas about dividing Bosnia and Herzegovina. In 1994 he quit the HDZ and founded his own party, the Independent Croatian Democrats (HND). Tudjman subsequently dismissed Mesić from his post in the Sabor.

Over the next several years Mesić became one of Tudjman's strongest critics. He ran for several political offices, but without success. After a few years in existence, the HND started to suffer from inner conflicts that ultimately led to a fatal split in 1997. Mesić then joined a middle of the road political association, the Croatian People's Party (HNS). The veteran statesman became a prominent voice in the HNS, serving as its executive vice president.

Many Croats and others were surprised when Mesić was elected president in 2000. The nation's new leader quit the HND, declaring himself unaffiliated. He explained that he wanted to be regarded as the president of all the citizens of Croatia. Polls have shown Mesić to be a truly popular president.

Separating himself from his predecessor and former ally Franjo Tudjman, Mesić declared in 2001,

> There was a lag in democratic development during President Tudjman's rule. He did not appreciate the European trends. He didn't understand democracy. He didn't understand history. Europe was uniting and he failed to understand this fact. He didn't understand the benefits that all the countries in a united Europe enjoyed through such an association.
>
> Now the Croatian policies have changed. We looked to European integration. We have left this period of isolation for the country. We are promoting democratic processes and establishing democratic institutions in the country.

Croatia's president, Stipe Mesić (Courtesy Office of the President of the Republic of Croatia)

membership is composed of ethnic Serbs who feel the best way to improve their conditions is to stay a part of Croatia and work within the system. A smaller Serb-dominated party is the Independent Serb Democratic Party (SSDS), which was formed in April 1997 and believes Eastern Slavonia should remain part of Croatia.

Like the SNS and SDSS, the Istrian Democratic Assembly (IDS) is an outlet for ethnic Croats. In this case, the population of Istria supports the federalization of Croatia. One other party, the small Croatian People's Party (HNS), was founded in 1990 and is centrist in tone. President Stipe Mesić was a member, and his election to the nation's top office has given the HNS a bit more clout politically. It does not play a major role on the Croatian national stage.

Human Rights and the United Nations War Crimes Tribunal

At the end of World War II, an international body for the prosecution of war crimes was established, and war crimes courts were held in Nuremberg, Germany, and Tokyo, Japan. When incidents of ethnic cleansing were initially reported in the Balkan civil war of 1991–95, the United Nations decided to follow the example set 45 years earlier, and on May 25, 1993, the UN Security Council passed Resolution 827 establishing the International Criminal Tribunal for the Former Yugoslavia (ICTY).

ICTY is based in The Hague, Netherlands, and has jurisdiction for persons accused of war crimes, crimes against humanity, and genocide in the former Yugoslavia occurring since January 1, 1991. The tribunal does not maintain a police force, so it is dependent on police in the former Yugoslav republics, other states, or international peace forces such as UNPROFOR to make arrests and turn over suspects.

Croatia has had a mixed record in cooperation with the ICTY. In November 2000, the ICTY's chief prosecutor accused Croatia of not turning over requested documents. Then in June 2001 opponents to the Mesić government insisted that Croatia stop cooperating with the ICTY after the ICTY issued indictments against two Croatian generals, Rahim Ademi and Ante Gotovina. Ademi was indicted for 38 murders, com-

Franjo Tudjman answers questions to foreign reporters on October 18, 1999, regarding the extradition of Croatian army generals requested by the International War Crimes Tribunal. (AP/Wide World Photos/Hrvoje Knez)

mitted by troops under his command near Gospić in 1993. Gotovina was indicted for murder, house destruction, and other abuses against Croatian Serbs in 1995.

The Mesić government survived a vote of no confidence in May 2001 and without the pressure of political opponents decided to resume full cooperation with the ICTY. Ademi surrendered to the ICTY in July, while Gotovina is at large. According to the ICTY rules, suspects cannot be tried in absentia (if they are not present in the courtroom), so a search for Gotovina is in effect.

A prominent watchdog group, Human Rights Watch (HRW), publicly commended the Croatian government for turning over Ademi and Gotovina to the ICTY. In a letter to Croatian prime minister Ivica Račan dated July 13, 2001, two of HRW's directors praised the Mesić government, saying, "We are aware that, in the past, Croatia has cooperated with the tribunal regarding the provision of documents, access to witnesses and sites of crimes, exhumations, and the surrender of Bosnian Croat indictees present in Croatia, but the ultimate test is the surrender of the country's own nationals if they are indicted. . . . We urge continued support for those efforts. Only through such steps toward accountability can Croatia confirm its democratic transition and prospects for European integration."

At the same time, the ICTY demonstrated fairness by charging Serbian leaders for similar crimes committed against Croatia during the war. These included four members of the Yugoslav People's Army and Navy as well as former Serbian president Slobodan Milošević.

However, according to a HRW report in October 2002, Croatia has not fulfilled its promise to turn over indicted people. In addition to Gotovina, a retired general named Janko Bobetko is wanted for war crimes against Croatian Serbs. While Gotovina is supposedly at large, Croatian government officials have claimed that they will not turn over Bobetko since "he was only doing his constitutional duty to protect Croatia's territorial integrity."

In response, HRW's regional executive director Elizabeth Anderson stated, "The real test of Croatia's commitment to international justice comes with these hard cases, involving its own wartime leadership. At the moment, it looks like they are failing that test."

NOTES

p. 59 "The Republic of Croatia is a . . ." "The Constitution of the Republic of Croatia." Available on-line. URL: http://www.usud.hr/html/the_constitution_of_the_republ.htm. Downloaded on January 30, 2003.

p. 59 "Freedom, equal rights, national equality . . ." "The Constitution of the Republic of Croatia." Available on-line. URL: http://www.usud.hr/html/the_constitution_of_the_republ.htm. Downloaded on January 30, 2003.

p. 62 "The millenary identity of the Croatian nation . . ." "The Constitution of the Republic of Croatia." Available on-line. URL: http://www.usud.hr/html/the_constitution_of_the_republ.htm. Downloaded on January 30, 2003.

p. 65 "Together, the HKDU and HSP won . . ." Croatia Net. "Political System." Available on-line. URL: http://www.croatia.net/html/politics.html. Downloaded on February 2, 2003.

p. 67 "'There was a big lag in democratic development . . .'" International Special Reports. "President Stjepan Mesić: Signaling a maturation of Croation democracy," International Special Reports website. Available on-line. URL: http://www.internationalspecialreports.com/europe/01/croatia/president.html. Downloaded on February 2, 2003.

pp. 69–70 "'We are aware that, in the past . . .'" Human Rights Watch. "HRW Letter to Croatian Prime Minister Ivica Racan." July 13, 2001, Human Rights

Watch website. Available on-line. URL: http://www.hrw.org/press/2001/07/croatia0713-ltr.htm. Downloaded on January 30, 2003.

p. 70 "'he was only doing his constitutional duty . . .'" Human Rights Watch. "Croatia Failing Test on War Crimes Accountability." October 2, 2002, Human Rights Watch website. Available on-line. URL: http:/hrw.org/press/2002/10/croatia1002.htm. Downloaded on January 31, 2003.

p. 70 "'The real test of Croatia's commitment . . .'" Human Rights Watch. "Croatia Failing Test on War Crimes Accountability."

5

RELIGION

Unlike Bosnia and Herzegovina, its highly diverse neighbor to the south, Croatia is dominated by one religion, Catholicism. According to the last national census, taken in 2001, almost 3.9 million, or nearly 88 percent of the population. is Catholic. The next most populous religion is Eastern Orthodoxy, with roughly 4.5 percent of the whole. There are also smaller minorities of Muslims, Jews, Protestants, and atheists.

Catholicism

While the Roman Catholic Church does receive some state support, such as direct subsidies and partial funding for the salaries of Catholic religious leaders, there is no official state religion in the republic. However, that line separating church and state was often blurred during the Tudjman presidency, whose HDZ went out of its way to identify itself with the Catholic Church. Since the ascendancy of Stipe Mesić, the climate for religious tolerance has improved.

The roots of Catholicism in Croatia were planted almost 14 centuries ago. It is believed that the first contact between Croats and the church was in 641, when a representative of the Vatican, Abbot Martin, journeyed to Croatia to redeem the remains of Christian martyrs and slaves. Over the next two centuries a gradual baptism into the Catholic Church of these early Croats took place. In 879, the Croats' ruler, Branimir, pledged his loyalty and allegiance to the church in a letter he sent to

Pope John VIII. The pope responded in a letter dated June 7, 879, that he had invoked God's blessing on Branimir's land as he celebrated mass at St. Peter's grave in Rome.

For a long time Croatia had an unusual privilege in its relationship with the Roman Catholic Church. In the ninth century, Pope Innocent IV granted the Croatian Church the right to conduct worship ceremonies in the Croats' national language and alphabet as opposed to the usually required Latin, making Croatia the only nation permitted to do so until the Second Vatican Council, also known as Vatican II, took place from 1962 through 1965.

During the centuries when much of Croatia was part of the Ottoman Empire, a small number of Croats converted to Islam or Christian Orthodoxy. The remaining Catholics did their best to preserve their religious beliefs and identity. Under Austria-Hungary in the second half of the 19th and early 20th centuries, Catholicism flourished as Croat university students and intellectuals reacted to the dormancy of the Ottoman years by actively trying to introduce Catholic principles and religious ideas into everyday society.

The 20th century has seen Croatian attitudes towards Catholicism go full circle from the aforementioned religious pride to a doctrine of religious supremacy to official atheism to a celebration of everyday public practice. It was during the 1930s and early 1940s, and especially during World War II, that the fascist Ustaša, which identified with the Catholic Church, distorted Catholic beliefs to justify purging and brutalizing religious minorities, especially Jews and Orthodox Serbs.

So it is natural that much of the Croatian Catholic population spent the post-war era in self-reflection, looking back on the Ustaša's actions and not flaunting their religion. That would have been difficult anyway, since communism, even the more liberalized form under Tito, was an officially atheistic ideology. Catechism, or the instruction of Christian tenets, was no longer permitted in schools, and the government did all it could to block the building of new churches. Diplomatic relations to the Vatican were cut, and atheism was encouraged.

Official relations between Croatia and the Vatican were restored in 1966, but atheism continued as the official state policy. It did little, however, to dampen the religious spirit of Catholic Croats, whose ethnic identity is intertwined with their religion. In 1979, Catholic Croats embarked on a pilgrimage to Rome with the intent of presenting to Pope John Paul II a written renewal of Croatian baptismal vows. The pope held Mass for the pilgrims. As a show of solidarity, the mass was given not in Latin but in Croatian.

After Croatia declared its independence in 1991, the Vatican was the first foreign state to recognize the new nation. During the civil war ethnic cleansing took place on the parts of both Catholic Croats and Orthodox Croatian Serbs, with houses of worship and other religious properties destroyed on both sides. Even though the war ended in 1995, violent incidents have continued, especially by Catholics toward Eastern Orthodox Christians in troubled Eastern Slavonia.

To realize how much religion plays a role in the Croats' daily lives, consider that in July 2000 the Catholic Church and the government-operated Croatian State Radio and Television (HRT) signed a formal agreement to provide regular coverage of Catholic events. There is only one private national radio station in Croatia, and it is operated by the Catholic Church (it is run by private, not state, financing).

In addition, the government requires religious training to be offered in public schools. Attendance is not mandatory, and if there is a minimum of seven minority students in a class, separate instruction is offered for those students. However, since there are few qualified teachers of minority religions in the republic and few resources, Catholic catechism is commonly the only religious instruction given.

Eastern Orthodoxy

To understand the conflicts between Roman Catholic and Eastern Orthodox Christians, it is helpful to consider some of the history of this minority religion in Croatia. Eastern Orthodox Christianity is an offshoot of Catholicism. Its beginnings date to the fourth century A.D., when Roman emperor Constantine the Great converted to Christianity. Following his conversion, he moved his capital to the site of present-day Istanbul, Turkey. In ancient times the city had been called Byzantium, but Constantine named it after himself: Constantinople.

The two religions have since had many disputes, despite the fact that both Croats and Serbs are descendants of the same Slavonic peoples.

Probably the largest source of disagreement is that Eastern Orthodox Christians do not accept the authority of the pope. In addition, Eastern Orthodox Christians allow priests to marry.

It is thought that today's Eastern Orthodox residents of Croatia are descendents of refugees from Serbia from the days when the Ottoman Empire ruled the region. Most were settled around Knin and along the Sava River by the Hapsburgs. Because they served as a buffer against the Turks, they were given the notable privileges of freedom to practice their own religion and freedom from serfdom.

The continuing disputes between Croatia's Catholics and Orthodox Christians has been compared by many to the constant conflicts between Catholics and Protestants in Ireland. Here are two groups who share the same ethnic background and language, but who are divided by religion,

Years after the fighting ended, the refugee problem has yet to go away. At right, a Croatian Serb who fled Croatia bathes his child in a refugee camp outside Belgrade in June 2002. (AP/Wide World Photos/Darko Vojinovic)

or as some believe, a combination of religion and nationhood. Orthodox churches continue to be vandalized, and church officials have reported that Orthodox priests, recognizable because of their unique clerical garments, do not feel safe walking the streets of their parishes because of repeated harassment. In spite of those problems, life for Eastern Orthodox Christians in Croatia is significantly easier under Stipe Mesić than when Franjo Tudjman was president. The 2001 census did show a troubling trend, however. According to the 1991 census, roughly 600,000 Eastern Orthodox Serbs lived in Croatia, but the 2001 census showed that only about 196,000, or about 4.5 percent of the population, live there now.

Prominent Croatian Serbs publicly wondered about the decrease of more than 400,000 Serb Orthodox Croatians. A spokesman for the Serb National Council, Milorad Pupovac, suggested that many ethnic Serbs did not tell the truth on their census forms, fearing ongoing hostility in the republic. He also accused Croatia's National Bureau of Statistics of purposely underestimating the Serb population by excluding about 130,000 Serb refugees yet to return from Serbia.

Representatives of human rights groups tended to agree with the figures, suggesting that many Serbian Orthodox Christians left Croatia as part of the republic's ethnic cleansing programs during the war. Most left in two waves, first in 1991 when Croatia declared its independence, and then in 1995 when breakaway areas such as Eastern Slavonia were recaptured by Croatia. Experts also believe that many Croatian citizens involved in mixed Serbo-Croatian marriages now refer to themselves as Croats for fear of discrimination.

Islam

Although evidence exists that Muslims have lived in eastern Croatia since the 10th century, it was the entrance of the Ottoman Turks that made Islam a major religion in the Balkans during the 14th through 16th centuries. Since so many Bosnians willingly converted to Islam, their Ottoman rulers allowed them to serve as professionals and important government officials.

Islam was founded by the prophet Muhammad in the city of Mecca, in what is now the sheikdom of Saudi Arabia, in the A.D. 600s. Muslims believe in one god named Allah, which means "the God." Muslims practice five pillars of worship: *shahada,* or the acceptance and confirmation of Allah as the one and only God; prayer; almsgiving, or helping the poor; fasting, which Muslims practice from sunrise to sunset everyday during the month of Ramadan, the ninth month of the Islamic calendar; and *hadj,* or pilgrimage, since the Islamic holy book, the Qur'an, commands all physically and financially healthy Muslims to make a journey to Mecca.

Muslims believe Islam is a continuation of the teachings of all prophets since the time of Abraham. While a fundamentalist and violent form of Islam has been growing strongly in much of the Arab world—as well as in non-Arab nations such as Iran and Pakistan—it has not taken hold in the Balkans. Unlike the majority of Muslim countries, Muslim women in Croatia have the same basic rights as men. Also, Muslim women in Croatia are not required to wear a burka, a tent-like covering that conceals their entire bodies. Still, everything is not completely equal for Muslim women. Their society by custom is generally patriarchal, and they tend to live in the same region as the oldest male household member's family.

According to the 2001 census, there are just under 57,000 Muslims in Croatia. Muslims here have had a long, unusual relationship with resident Catholics. They were spared genocide at the hands of the Ustaša during World War II, since the Ustaša viewed them as Croatian Catholics who had rejected Catholicism. Since the Ustaša believed they were Catholics by nature, they were not forced to convert, as the Serbs and others were. Indeed, during the war many Muslims worked alongside the Ustaša.

At first, the Tito government saw Yugoslav Muslims as a group with no national identity, even though Muslims insisted they were a nationality in addition to a religious group. The League of Communists of Yugoslavia (LCY) changed its mind and in 1968 formally recognized them as a sixth Yugoslav nationality, along with Slovenians, Serbs, Croatians, Macedonians, and Montenegrins.

The Muslims of Bosnia and Herzegovina were victims of genocide during the civil war of the 1990s, as Serbia tried to clear them out of their homes. Over the course of the war, Muslims, Orthodox Serbs, and Croatian Catholics switched sides periodically, but for much of the time there was a strong Croat-Muslim alliance against the Serbs. Muslims and Catholics fought alongside each other for most of those horrible years. Today Croatia's Catholics and Muslims have generally friendly relations with one another. Like Catholics, Muslims are given radio broadcast time, but on Radio Zagreb as opposed to HRT. They are allowed one paid religious holiday from work and are allowed to take off work to care for others, although they do not get paid for those days.

Judaism

For much of 13 centuries, the Balkans have welcomed Jews, where as other lands—mainly those ruled by Christians who were hostile to non-Christians—have evicted them. Records show that Jews entered what is now Croatia in 723, after banishment from Constantinople. After a more famous expulsion, known as the Spanish Inquisition in 1492, Jews were forced to leave Spain, where they had been at home for centuries. They had to look for homes wherever they could, and many discovered that they were welcome in what are now the Croatian communities of Split and Dubrovnik.

In 1873, Croatia's Jews were afforded full civil rights, and they served as pillars of the nation, taking active roles in everything from art to education. According to various estimates, there were between 20,000 and 37,000 Jews living in Croatia between the world wars. That period of tolerance and prosperity ended when the Nazi-allied Ustaša embarked on their genocidal campaign against Jews and other minorities. It is estimated that 75 to 80 percent of the Jewish population of Croatia was killed in concentration camps, the worst being in Jasenovac.

Under the official atheistic policy of communism, the Jews, like other religions in Croatia, were encouraged not to practice religion. During the period from 1945 to 1990 there was no rabbi, or Jewish spiritual leader, in Zagreb, home of the republic's largest Jewish community.

According to the 2001 Croatian census, there are but 495 Jews in Croatia, today accounting for about .01 percent of the population. However, that may be a low figure since when asked on the official census form to declare one nationality, many selected a nonreligious one, such as Croat or Serb. Unofficial estimates by Jewish organizations put the Jew-

MESIĆ APOLOGIZES FOR HOLOCAUST CRIMES

The Holocaust against the Jews and other minorities during World War II continues to be emblematic of intolerance taken to an extreme, yet for a long time few representatives of countries that were responsible for the crimes took responsibility. Historians at Yad Vashem, Israel's Holocaust memorial, estimate that from 1941 to 1945 the Ustaša killed more than 500,000 people, expelled another 250,000, and forced 200,000 more to convert to Catholicism. The Ustaša murdered 30,000 Croatian Jews (about 80 percent of Croatia's Jewish population), 20,000 Roma (Gypsies), and thousands of their political opponents. Yet little of this had been acknowledged by Croatia's leaders since the war.

That is why a visit to Yad Vashem on October 31, 2001, by Croatia's president, Stipe Mesić, was unprecedented. While in Israel, Mesić asked for "forgiveness' from all those who were harmed by Croatians and, of course, first of all from the Jews."

After touring the Holocaust museum section of Yad Vashem, Mesić wrote in the guestbook, "The Holocaust is a crime the monstrosity of which has no parallel in the history of humankind. Whenever I come across its records, I ask myself, although I know the answer: was something like that truly possible? Filled with horror, I reply to myself: yes, it was!"

"We must not let ignorance replace the knowledge of the Holocaust in the awareness of the present and coming generations. We must know, so that what happened should never happen again."

"By visiting Yad Vashem I am paying homage to all the victims of the Holocaust with the message that their memory must never pale."

ish population in Croatia at about 2,000, spread throughout nine communities. Most live in Zagreb, but there are also synagogues or prayer rooms in Dubrovnik, Split, and Rijeka.

Jews are an officially recognized minority group, which means they are eligible for state aid. That has translated into funds to help build a retirement home and a kindergarten. Under Franjo Tudjman, there were some anti-Jewish feelings vocalized by the people of Croatia, including Tudjman himself. The former president wrote a book that downplayed the role of Croatians in the Holocaust, which is ironic considering that he fought in the resistance against the Ustaša and Nazis during World War II. After the publication of the book Tudjamn apologized to the Jewish people for his written words.

As with other religions, Jews have experienced more freedom under President Mesić. For example, Jewish topics are covered on the state radio network, HRT, especially during Jewish holidays. Nevertheless, while the Jews of Croatia now have religious freedom and are able to attend religious services without repercussion, the majority consider themselves cultural rather than religious Jews. Common activities include celebrating Shabbat (Sabbath) or other Jewish holidays with their families or at Jewish social clubs.

Other Religions

A smattering of various Protestant denominations exist in Croatia. They rarely get publicity. According to the 2001 census, there were 15 Methodists and 4,053 Calvinists. In addition, there were a few hundred to a few thousand Evangelic Christians, Seventh Day Adventists, Jehovah's Witnesses, Pentecostals, and Baptists. Also, about 132,500 Croatians labeled themselves agnostic or uncommitted, and a little over 98,000 said they were atheists.

Visiting the Holy Places of Croatia

Croatia's religious heritage manifests itself in its many religious shrines, including sites dating back to antiquity. Of the abundance of places visitors love to see, the following are among the most popular.

The towering twin spires of the Cathedral of the Assumption of the Blessed Virgin Mary in Zagreb date to 1899, almost brand new by Balkan standards. However, the church, long known as St. Stephen's Cathedral, contains many elements of the original medieval cathedral that stood on this spot. An 1880 earthquake destroyed much of the centuries-old structure, but still inside remain 13th century frescoes, Renaissance-period pews, and marble altars.

High on a hilltop in Rominj, a town in Istria, is the massive Church of St. Euphemia. It is the largest baroque-style building in Istria, and many people come just to admire the architecture. However, most religious Catholics come to visit the sixth-century Byzantine sarcophagus containing the remains of St. Euphemia herself, a patron saint of Rominj who lived in the third century. Legend has it that as a teenager in Constantinople Euphemia refused to renounce her Christian faith. As punishment she was put in a lion's den. The story goes that the lions killed her but refused to eat her body. Her remains were brought to Rominj around the year 800. Every September 16 pilgrims gather at her tomb on the anniversary of her death. A copper statue of St. Euphemia has been placed atop the church's bell tower.

Not far away is the 2,000-year-old town of Poreč, where the main attraction is the Euphrasian Basilica, declared by the United Nations Educational, Scientific and Cultural Organization (UNESCO) to be a World Heritage Site. It is one of 690 such sites judged to be so important and well preserved that it can never be altered in appearance in order that future generations will be able to enjoy it. The basilica, which dates to the sixth century, is a wonderful and rare example of early Christian architecture and is best known for its dazzling Byzantine gold mosaics of

Fresco from the Euphrasian Basilica in Poreč, dating from the sixth century (Courtesy Croatian National Tourist Office, New York)

Jesus and female saints. Sculptures in the basilica also date to the sixth century, while the remnants of a fourth century mosaic floor are also found in the complex.

Perhaps the largest concentration of historic religious structures is found in the grand seaport city of Dubrovnik. It is home to the second-oldest synagogue in Europe still in use, even though the Jewish population of Dubrovnik numbers just a few dozen people. (The oldest European synagogue is in Prague in the Czech Republic.) Dubrovnik's synagogue was built in the style of Italian medieval synagogues in the 14th century in the city's ancient Jewish quarter, and its current interior decoration was completed in 1652. The Holy Ark, which holds the Torah, or sacred scrolls, is decorated with woodcuts and mounted on gold painted pillars, while the Torah scrolls were brought from Spain by Jews escaping from the Spanish Inquisition, a religious tribunal established to punish Jewish and, later, Muslim converts to Christianity suspected of false conversion. The roof of the synagogue was damaged during the 1991 shelling but has since been repaired.

There are several important Christian sights in Dubrovnik, too. One is the Franciscan Monastery, originally constructed in 1337 but completely rebuilt after a 1667 earthquake. It is best known for two features not usually thought of in connection with churches. One is Europe's third-oldest pharmacy, located inside the monastery and dating to 1317. The other is an immense library with roughly 30,000 books and 1,500 rare handwritten documents, some dating to the 1400s.

Another Dubrovnik site is the Dominican Monastery. Built in increments between the 13th and 15th centuries, it is still home to Dominican monks. In various locations throughout the monastery are the graves of some of Dubrovnik's most important noble families as well as its craftsmen and merchants. A favorite pastime of visitors is wandering the building, from the nave to the cloisters, trying to read the faded inscriptions on the grave markers. Dubrovnik also has a small mosque where the city's 4,000 Muslims worship, and the nearby Serbian Orthodox Church, which by Dubrovnik standards is fairly new, dating to the 1800s.

One other religious shrine deserves mention, even though it is located just over the Croatian border in Bosnia and Herzegovina. To some Catholics, St. James Church in Medjugorje (pronounced "Med-yu-gor-yeh") is the location of a modern miracle. On June 24, 1981, six teenagers reported that the ghost of Jesus's mother, the Virgin Mary, appeared to them in Medjugorje. While the Catholic Church never officially verified the sightings, that has not stopped huge numbers of devout Croatian Catholics from making pilgrimages to Apparition Hill, the place where the Virgin Mary supposedly appeared. St. James Church, built in 1969, has become a kind of unofficial headquarters for these religious pilgrims.

NOTES

p. 72 "According to the last national census . . ." "Population by religion, by towns/municipalities, census 2001" Croatian Bureau of Statistics. Available on-line. URL: http://www.dzs.hr/Eng/Census/census2001.htm. Downloaded on February 4, 2003.

p. 72 "The next most populous religion . . ." "Population by religion, by towns/municipalities, census 2001." Downloaded on February 4, 2003.

p. 76 "The 2001 census did show a troubling trend . . ." *Balkantimes.com* "Croatia Census Finds Substantial Drop in Ethnic Serb Population," *Southern European Times*, June 17, 2002. Available on-line. URL: http://www.balkantimes.com/default3.asp?lang=english&page=process_print&arti cle_id=15788. Downloaded on February 4, 2003.

p. 77 "According to the 2001 census . . ." "Population by religion, by towns/municipalities, census 2001" Croatian Bureau of Statistics. Available on-line. URL: http://www.dzs.hr/Eng/Census/census2001.htm. Downloaded on February 4, 2003.

p. 78 "According to various estimates . . ." World Jewish Congress. "Jewish Communities of the World: Croatia," World Jewish Congress website. Available on-line. URL: http://www.wjc.org.il/wjcbook/croatia/. Downloaded on February 4, 2003 and Yad Vashem. "Croatian President Mesić Apologizes for Croatian Crimes Against Jews during the Holocaust," Yad Vashem press release. Available on-line. URL: http://www.yad-vashem.org.il/about_yad/press_room/press_releases/croatian_president.html. Downloaded on February 4, 2003.

p. 78 "According to the 2001 Croatian census . . ." Croatian Bureau of Statistics. "Population by religion, by towns/municipalities, census 2001" Croatian Bureau of Statistics. Available on-line. URL:http://www.dzs.hr/Eng/Census/census2001.htm. Downloaded on February 4, 2003.

p. 79 "The Ustaša murdered 30,000 Croatian Jews . . ." Yad Vashem. "Croatian President Mesić Apologizes for Croatian Crimes Against Jews during the Holocaust," Yad Vashem press release. Available on-line. URL: http://www.yad.vashem.org.il/about_yad/press_room/press_releases/croatian_president.html. Downloaded on February 4, 2003.

p. 79 "'forgiveness from all those . . .'" "Croatian President Mesić Apologizes for Croatian Crimes Against Jews during the Holocaust." Downloaded on February 4, 2003.

p. 79 "'The Holocaust is a crime . . .'" "Croatian President Mesić Apologizes for Croatian Crimes Against Jews during the Holocaust." Downloaded on February 4, 2003.

p. 80 "In addition, there were a few hundred . . ." Croatian Bureau of Statistics. "Population by religion, by towns/municipalities, census 2001." Croatian Bureau of Statistics. Available on-line. URL: http://www.dzs.hr/Eng/Census/census2001.htm. Downloaded on February 4, 2003.

p. 80 "Also, about 132,5000 Croatians . . ." "Population by religion, by town/municipalities, census 2001." Downloaded on February 4, 2003.

6

ECONOMY

Croatia has endured numerous roadblocks in attempting to build a healthy economy. The nation has had to undergo a considerable transition from a quasicommunist economy to a free market. Croatia has also had to endure a bloody war and the havoc that such a conflict brings to a nation, both emotionally and physically. Over the last several years, it has been necessary for the republic to deal with the major effort of reconstruction.

Background

When it was part of Yugoslavia, Croatia was the country's second most prosperous republic, behind only Slovenia. Under Titoism, Croatia changed from a heavily agricultural economy to a more diversified one, with an emphasis on industry, including textiles, chemicals, oil, machine tools, and ship building.

Indeed, Croatia had one of the most respected ship building industries in the world. From 1956 until 1990, Croatia delivered 745 ships of all kinds; 90 percent of them were purchased by other countries. In addition to crafting entire boats, the industry devoted much effort to repairing existing ships and manufacturing a wide range of ship equipment such as diesel engines, diesel generators, control panels, compressors, and deck cranes.

That is not to say that agriculture was not a major factor in bringing in money. About two-thirds of the republic's land was cultivated prior to the fall of Titoism. Top products included oats, rye, wheat, sugar beets, barley, potatoes, and corn. Out of ample orchards came apples, pears, plums, cherries, and olives, while livestock included pigs, poultry, cattle, and sheep.

Shipbuilding has been an important industry for centuries on the Dalmatian coast. This photograph shows shipbuilders in Split in 1955. (Courtesy United Nations)

Croatia also boasts a bountiful supply of natural resources, which not only serve its own people's needs but provides enough excess to be exported to other countries. Oil and natural gas are found in Eastern Slavonia, while Dalmatia and the Istrian Peninsula are rich with bauxite deposits. Sizable supplies of coal and smaller deposits of zinc, lead, iron, and salt can be found throughout the land.

Thanks to Croatia's long coastline, the republic is fortunate to harvest two different kinds of natural resources. One is seafood, as about 40 species of edible fish and shellfish are harvested commercially by Croatian fishermen. The other consists of the lovely beaches along the Adriatic Sea, which lure visitors from landlocked central European nations and form the foundation of Croatia's biggest source of foreign income: tourism.

As noted in chapter two, Titoism was a fairly unregulated type of communism. Businesses, even though they were under federal control, were generally allowed to set their own prices and compete with each other to a degree. In addition, workers had some input in their employers' business practices.

However, even with these compromises toward capitalism, the Titoist system was not a free market economy, and Croatia's economy, as part of Yugoslavia's, suffered from some of the same problems other communist countries did. There was gross mismanagement, with factories built as favors to politicians more concerned with shoring up their political images than making the best use of a region's natural resources. These became known informally as political factories. In addition, it was common for factories and other businesses to employ too many workers, including some whose positions were not necessary. This lack of efficiency translated into lower profits.

These problems, along with high inflation rates and stagnant growth in the 1980s, led to the purging of the Titoist system in the early 1990s and the drive toward a free market economy, but a complete turnaround in a nation's basic economic system means major changes. New laws must be made, and old habits must be altered, which takes time. A Ministry of Privatization was established in Croatia's government in order to help smooth the transition to a free market economy. Laws passed in Croatia allowed employees to purchase stock shares in the newly privatized companies. Foreign investment was gratefully accepted.

While this change to capitalism was not easy for any of the former communist nations of eastern Europe, it was immensely more difficult in the former Yugoslavia. Just as the drive toward building a free market economy had begun, war broke out.

The priorities for Croatians changed from earning livings to saving their lives. Damage to property was devastating. Much of the nation's infrastructure was ruined. It is estimated that about 30 percent of Croatia's electricity-generating capacity was destroyed. Severe damage was also done to bridges, roads, and railroad tracks (which halted transportation), as well as to factories and refineries (which stopped production). Agriculture suffered because much of the land was scarred. Although the Dalmatian Coast was the scene of only limited fighting over the course of the war, tourists did not want to chance trips to the Adriatic coast. The lucrative tourist industry was suddenly stagnant.

The net result was a huge trade imbalance and a burdensome cost of rebuilding at the war's end. It is estimated that from 1989 to 1993 Croatia's gross domestic product fell 40.5 percent. The total cost of economic loss in Croatia due to the war has been estimated at $27.5 billion, more than a year's gross domestic product (GDP) for the republic.

Foreign Aid

Experts in international finance knew there was no way the Republic of Croatia could get back on its feet by itself. Many nations, either on their own or through organizations such as the World Bank, have aided Croatia by providing millions of dollars in assistance to help rebuild the broken nation, including funds for food and emergency assistance, peace-keeping assistance, and technical cooperation. At the forefront is the United States, which acts mainly through a government agency called The United States Agency for International Development (USAID).

However, USAID is hardly the only source of foreign investment. Immediately after the war ended, other countries lending a significant helping hand to Croatia included Germany, Switzerland, Sweden, Austria, and Belgium. Much of the money was allocated toward rebuilding industries, including telecommunications, electronics, breweries, and

USAID

USAID has been around since the end of World War II. With much of Europe decimated after four years of carnage, President Harry Truman's secretary of state, George Marshall, devised a plan to rebuild Europe by paying for much of its reconstruction. While altruism might have been the professed aim of the plan, an intended benefit was good relations between the United States and the affected nations after the reconstruction was complete. In some countries, especially Greece and Turkey, the plan worked, and those two nations have been strongly allied with the United States ever since. In 1961, President John F. Kennedy changed the Marshall Plan from a one-time program to a regular U.S. policy when he signed into law the Foreign Assistance Act, which created USAID.

In the case of Croatia, USAID agreed to send financial assistance in 1995, shortly after the war had ended. In doing so, USAID made clear to the people of Croatia that simply sending their nation American money would not be enough. Everyone from private business to government to the media to private citizens has had to do their part to rebuild their nation.

The agency summarized its intent by stating,

> USAID's goal in Croatia is to help the country make a successful transition to a democratic society and a market economy and, in so doing, serve as a cornerstone for stability in the region. In order to achieve this goal, governance at all levels must become more transparent, efficient and responsive to citizens' needs. Citizens must maintain a high level of participation in enacting change and improving their communities. Finally, independent media organizations must hold all levels of government accountable, while providing citizens with the balanced information they need to participate effectively in a democratic society. Additional assistance will be provided at the central level to introduce and shore-up reform as needs and partners are identified, with much of the national support linking to local developments.

With an estimated completion date of 2006, USAID began its recovery program in 1995. At first, the news was good. According to the World Bank, which itself began aiding Croatia as early as the fall of 1993, the stabilization program began as one of the most successful such programs in eastern Europe. Between 1994 and 1998 only Poland and the Slovak Republic grew faster than Croatia among eastern European nations.

construction materials. Much foreign money from Europe, as well as international agencies such as the World Bank and the International Monetary Fund (IMF), has come in the form of humanitarian aid.

Total foreign aid to Croatia has been on the upswing. In 2000, foreign aid totaled $66 million, up from $54 million five years earlier. While that might sound like a lot of money, it is significantly less than the total amounts sent to countries such as China, Egypt, Bangladesh, and Croatia's neighbors Serbia and Montenegro, which total well over a billion dollars each. Additionally, in 2000 foreign aid totaled just 0.4 percent of Croatia's gross national income (GNI). By comparison, foreign aid to Serbia and Montenegro in 2000 totaled 13.4 percent of that nation's gross national income, an indication of the nation's dependence on outside money.

USAID has reported that in the mid-1990s Croatia was viewed as one of the richest nations in eastern Europe and the most advanced among

RON BROWN AND CROATIA

Considering his background, Ron Brown seems an unlikely hero for the Croatian people. An African-American man, Ronald H. Brown was born in Washington, D.C., and grew up as the son of a hotel manager in the predominantly black New York City neighborhood of Harlem.

After earning a law degree and working in Democratic Party politics, Brown served as President Bill Clinton's secretary of commerce. After the signing of the Dayton Peace Agreement, Brown became actively involved in rebuilding the war-torn nations of the former Yugoslavia. Just months after the talks at Dayton, Brown and his staff embarked on an official business trip to the Balkans to assess the potential of investing over $5 billion of American capital in the area as part of a reconstruction system. His plan was similar to the Marshall Plan following World War II. The Americans were considering putting their funds towards a rebuilding of Croatia's and Bosnia's energy systems, transportation systems, homes, and health care facilities.

Brown and his staff started their endeavor on April 2, 1996, by flying from Paris to Tuzla in Bosnia and Herzegovina. After meeting with Bosnian businessmen, Brown and the others took off on a flight to Dubrovnik, Croatia, on April 3, with plans to meet with Croatian leaders. Heavy rains southeastern European countries in implementing economic policy reforms through arrangements with international financial institutions. Privatization, at least among small scale businesses, was completed early, and most trade restrictions were removed.

However, in the latter part of the 1990s, the Croatian economy slowed. USAID suspended work in financial sector reform in 1997 after an assessment indicated that the Tudjman government was showing little effort toward continuing economic reforms. Although, overall, foreign aid increased between 1995 and 2000, things got worse as the decade drew to a close. Political favoritism and a lack of reform legislation on the part of the government was blamed. The restructuring of government-owned businesses was slow to happen, and the supervision of Croatia's banks was weak. However, observers did not lay the blame solely on the politicians. Citizens, especially members of trade unions,

and strong winds hampered the pilot's ability to see, and at 2:52 P.M. the airplane disappeared off radar screens. After five hours of searching, rescuers found the wreckage of the plane near a mountaintop.

A program that granted European graduate students fellowships to study in the United States had been established in 1994. It was called simply the Central and Eastern European Graduate Fellowship Program. In 1996 it was officially renamed the Ron Brown Fellowship Program, as a reflection of Brown's commitment to building democracy in the region and strengthening the global economy.

On April 3, 1997, a year to the day after the crash that killed Brown and his staff, Croatia's ambassador to the United States, Miomir Žužul, said at a memorial ceremony,

> We in Croatia have come to know and value Ron Brown as a true friend during his tireless efforts to promote trade and investment in our region, and to help us rebuild our economy ravaged by years of aggression. Ron Brown understood, perhaps better than any of us, that democracy and economic opportunity are closely linked and that liberty and equality can best be sustained by an expanding, vibrant economy that offers genuine opportunities. The people of Croatia will never forget his efforts on our behalf.

hesitated to encourage reform for fear that privatization would cut jobs, wages, and benefits.

The Current Economic Situation

By the middle of 1998, Croatia was in a recession, which deepened in 1999 as budget expenditures exceeded revenue, leading to a federal deficit. Croatia's gross domestic production in 1999 was only 78 percent of its level 10 years earlier, and industrial production in 1999 was about 40 percent lower than its 1989 level.

Croatia's economic doldrums began to dissipate in 2000, and Stipe Mesić's new government has been given a considerable amount of credit. The Mesić leadership has made an effort to enact reform legislation. In a major policy switch, it has greatly reduced support for ethnic Croats living in Bosnia and Herzegovina, an expensive policy practiced by Tudjman that cost Croatia millions of dollars every year. In response, bilateral donors and international financial institutions have broadened their financial support of Croatia.

Since Mesić took office Croatia's gross domestic product (GDP) has steadily increased. In 2001 it grew 3.8 percent over that of 2000, and in 2002 it is estimated that the GDP was roughly three percent over 2001. Along the same lines, industrial production has gradually increased, and inflation has dropped from 6.2 percent in 2000 to roughly 3.2 percent in 2002.

This is not to say Croatia has completely recovered from the down times of the 1990s. For example, the official unemployment rate, 22 percent, is still high. Some economic experts warn not to take that figure too seriously, because of what is called by some the gray economy and by others the shadow economy. These are two terms for business conducted by companies that shun registration in order to evade payment of taxes. Some businesses consider the taxes exorbitant and avoid complying with government regulations.

Even taking the gray economy into account, a recent USAID analysis conceded that the unemployment rate is still too high, and the republic's greatest challenge is to generate new jobs for two main reasons: to absorb workers who lost existing jobs due to privatization, and to keep capable young people from leaving the country to look for better paying and more promising work elsewhere.

Another significant concern is the growth of Croatia's public debt. Due to slower than expected privatization and lingering government bureaucracy, foreign investment remains relatively low. Some reports say that other nations are also hesitant to invest in Croatia because of perceived corruption, especially in the Croatian court system. According to a USAID report, corruption could be tackled more effectively by simply enforcing existing laws. However, it appears to many that foreign investment, especially from Western nations, is the key to bolstering Croatia's economy. Promotion of tourism and further development of the oil industry are also vital to economic recovery.

Another problem is the lingering difficulties of converting from Titoism to privatization. Even though it has been well over a decade since communism in eastern Europe was toppled, there is still a high number of state-owned businesses in Croatia. Privately owned businesses are failing at a rapid pace, productivity is lower than expected, and the foreign debt at more than $10 billion continues to increase.

Poverty

While Croatia has continued to have some problems trying to return to a robust economy, it is not a nation steeped in poverty. As of 2001, the last time a study of poverty and income distribution in Croatia was conducted, its per capita income was the equivalent of $4,500, second-highest of the six former Yugoslav republics. Its life expectancy rate (70.5 years for men, 78 years for women), infant mortality rates (7.1 per 1,000 live births), and literacy rate (97 percent) are comparable to those of wealthier nations. However, that does not mean that Croatia is free of poverty.

Croatia's poor account for 8.4 percent of the total population. Contrary to common images, most poor people in Croatia are not homeless. They tend to reside in overcrowded and decrepit homes. The vast majority are poorly educated and live on unhealthy diets, especially those living in cities where food is more expensive. Most poor city dwellers can afford little more than potatoes, bread, and milk. Most have nothing in savings. Many get assistance from family members.

SETTING SAIL IN DUBROVNIK

The nature of Dubrovnik is defined by the sea. Located on the shore of the shiny Adriatic, Dubrovnik was a center of trade for much of its history, a prime link between the cities of the East and West. Through much of the latter half of the 20th century, Dubrovnik was regarded by serious and weekend sailors alike as a city of leisure, a base for sailing expeditions around the harbor or up and down the coast. People from Italy and central Europe came here to rent boats.

The civil war of the 1990s changed all that. During the shelling of 1991 nearly all of the sailing fleet was destroyed. Even if it had not

The natural harbors and well-equipped marinas of the South Adriatic attract sailboat enthusiasts, including vacationers and competitors in world-class regattas. (Courtesy Croatian National Tourist Office, New York)

been, the threat of violence was enough to keep people away. It has taken time, but Dubrovnik's seaside industry is recovering.

The manager of the Dubrovnik Marina, Dražen Čaleta, said in 2002, "After the war we started from nothing but succeeded in renovating the marina in just two years. We had to start with lower prices and have now increased to the normal level."

Leisure sailors began returning in 1997. By 2002 the business had grown to its prewar level. The world's largest charter company, Sunsail, has since relocated to Dubrovnik and now has more yachts in the area waters than it did before 1991. Business seems promising as foreign investors increasingly express interest in starting new boating enterprises in Dubrovnik. The city's mayor, Dubravka Šuica, reported in 2002, "Everyday I have someone coming from Europe and America trying to talk to me because they want to invest here. We are on the way to building a brand new marina."

Also contrary to what outsiders might think, poverty in Croatia is not limited to ethnic minorities. While it is true that minorities, Serbs, and especially Bosnian Muslims in Slavonia have generally higher poverty rates, most poor are Croats who fall into two categories: people with little education and the elderly. Almost three-fourths of the poor live in families whose head has only primary school education or no education at all. The second-biggest segment of poor people in Croatia are elderly people with little or no pension, or retirement, benefits. About 40 percent of the poor live in households with a retired head-of-household.

Financial experts from the World Bank have several recommendations to lessen poverty in the emerging republic. One is to improve the governance framework for businesses to make it easier for lower-income people to invest in stocks. Another, already implemented to a degree, is to reduce taxes on labor, to improve competitiveness, and to create an environment for job creation. A third is to encourage the creation of part-time working arrangements while enforcing a minimum level of regulations to ensure workers' rights, including sick leave, limited work hours, protection from harassment and discrimination, and workplace safety.

Continued Outside Help

As Croatia makes a concerted effort to become part of the European Union (EU), financial help is on its way. The World Bank has continued to initiate projects to get Croatia back on its feet. In the decade 1993–2003, the World Bank lent Croatia $1,065 billion to finance or cofinance 21 rebuilding operations.

One of the more recent projects, called the Renewable Energy Resource Project in Croatia, was signed on February 19, 2003. Its purpose is twofold: to reduce pollution and at the same time give a boost to the nation's ailing economy. According to a World Bank press release, the grant will help develop "an economically and environmentally sustainable market for renewable energy sources in Croatia. Development of this market will make Croatia's economy less reliant on imported electricity and fossil fuels, reduce emissions, and create an attractive climate for private investment in renewable energy, and generate local industry and employment."

A second significant recent World Bank project is the Country Economic Memorandum (CEM), a study of both key sectors of the Croatian economy and possible reforms with the intention of bringing Croatia closer to membership in the European Union. Part of the study, conducted in late 2002, indicated that there were delays in the disbursement of World Bank funds allocated toward four infrastructure projects, including ones to modernize Croatian railways and to reconstruct Eastern Slavonia. Despite that, the World Bank is optimistic that Croatia, under Stipe Mesić, will make best use of its funding assistance.

Interestingly, despite the economic woes since Croatian independence, most Croats still believe breaking off from Yugoslavia in 1991 was the right move. Ivan Smolić, a metal worker, conceded, "I have just left half of my salary in the bank to cover household bills. But everything has a price and I would settle for even lower standards just to have a state."

NOTES

p. 85 "From 1956 until 1990, Croatia delivered . . ." Croatia Your Partner. "The Shipbuilding Industry," Croatia: Your Partner website. Available on-line http://www.hgk.hr/cro_partner/adriatic/tekstovi/shipyard/shipyard.html. Downloaded on February 6, 2003.

p. 88 "It is estimated that about 30 percent . . . "Croatia," *The Europa World Year Book,* Volume 1, (London: Europa Publications, 2000), p. 1,149.

p. 88 "It is estimated that from 1989 to 1993 . . ." Bureau of European-Eurasian Affairs. "Background Note: Croatia" U.S. Department of State website, Bureau of European and Eurasian Affairs, April 2002. Available on-line. URL: http://www.state.gov/r/pa/ei/bgn/3166.htm. Downloaded on January 31, 2003.

p. 88 "The total cost of economic loss . . ." World Bank. "Croatia: Economic Vulnerability and Welfare Study," Document of World Bank, April 18, 2001. Available on-line. URL: http://wwwwds.worldbank.org/servlet/WDSContentServer/ WDSP/IB/2001/05/11/00009494 6 . . . Downloaded on February 7, 2003.

p. 89 "'USAID's goal in Croatia is to . . .'" USAID. "Croatia: Activity Data Sheet," The United States Agency for International Development website. Available on-line URL: http://www.usaid.gov/pubs/cbj2002/ee/hr/160-021.html. Downloaded on February 7, 2003.

p. 90 "Total foreign aid to Croatia . . ." Personal Correspondence from Naomi Halewood, Development Data Group, World Bank, April 30, 2003.

p. 90 "While that might sound like a lot . . ." Halewood.

p. 90 "Additionally, in 2000 . . ." Halewood.

p. 90 "By comparison, foreign aid . . ." Halewood.

p. 91 "'We in Croatia have come to know . . .'" "Croatian Ambassador Addresses 'Celebration of Lives' ceremony honoring Secretary Ron Brown and his mission," Embassy of Republic of Croatia to the United States of America Office of Public Affairs press release, April 3, 1997. Available on-line. URL: http://www. croatiaemb.org/news/Press_Releases/1997/press03qpr97.htm. Downloaded on February 10, 2003.

p. 92 "Croatia's gross domestic product . . ." World Bank "Croatia: Economic Vulnerability and Welfare Study."

p. 92 "In 2001 it grew 3.8 percent . . ." USAID. "Croatia: Overview, FY 2003 Congressional Budget Justification," The United States Agency for International Development website. Available on-line. URL: http://www.usaid.gov/ country/ee/hr. Downloaded February 7, 2003.

p. 92 "Along the same lines, industrial production . . ." Auswartiges Amt. "Croatia economy," Auswartiges Amt website. Available on-line. URL: http:// www.auswaertiges-amt.de. Downloaded on March 8, 2003.

p. 92 "For example, the official unemployment rate . . ." "Croatia economy."

p. 93 "As of 2001, the last time a study . . ." World Bank. "Croatia: Economic Vulnerability and Welfare Study."

p. 93 "Its life expectancy rate . . ." *The World Almanac and Book of Facts 2003,* (New York: World Almanac Books, 2003), p. 776.

p. 93 "Croatia's poor account for . . ." World Bank. "Croatia: Economic Vulnerability and Welfare Study."

p. 95 "Almost three-fourths of the poor . . ." "Croatia: Economic Vulnerability and Welfare Study."

p. 95 "'After the war we started from nothing . . .'" CNN "Croatia sails for tourist boom," CNN website, July 17, 2002. Available on-line. URL: http://www.cnn.com/2002/WORLD/sailing/07/17/croatia.biz/index.html. Downloaded on February 6, 2003.

p. 95 "'Everyday I have someone coming . . .'" "Croatia sails for tourist boom." Downloaded on February 6, 2003.

p. 95 "The second-biggest segment of poor people . . ." "Croatia: Economic Vulnerability and Welfare Study."

p. 96 "In the decade from 1993–2003 . . ." Bulic, Petra. "World Bank: Strategy and Projects in Croatia," World Bank website, January 24, 2003. Available on-line. URL: www.worldbank.hr/ECA/Croatia.nsf . . . Downloaded on March 8, 2003.

p. 96 "'an economically and environmentally sustainable . . .'" World Bank "Croatia and World Bank Sign Grant for Renewable Energy Resource Project," World Bank website, February 19, 2003. Available on-line. URL: www.worldbank.hr/ECA/Croatia.nsf . . . Downloaded on March 8, 2003.

p. 96 "Interestingly, despite the economic woes . . ." British Broadcasting Corporation. "Croatia and Slovenia mark anniversary," BBC website, January 15, 2002. Available on-line URL: news.bbc.co.uk/l/hi/world/Europe/1762001.stm. Downloaded on March 8, 2003.

p. 96 "'I have just left half of my salary . . .'" "Croatia and Slovenia mark anniversary." Downloaded on March 8, 2003.

7

CULTURE

If a single word sums up the Croats' attitude toward their cultural traditions and institutions, it is pride. Croatian culture—from music to visual arts—has had a long history, dating back over 1,000 years.

Music

Croatia's musical heritage, like that of most of Europe, begins with the Catholic Church in the Middle Ages. The first transcripts of church music in Croatia date to the 11th century, and some folk tunes written in the 12th century to celebrate the birth of Jesus are still popular at Christmas today. Among the earliest musical groups in Dubrovnik was one formed in the 15th century for the sole purpose of celebrating the holiday honoring Dubrovnik's patron saint, St. Blasius.

Croatian composers contributed much to the Renaissance taking place in Italy across the Adriatic Sea in the 16th century. One of the best-known Croatian composers from the era was Julije Skjavetić, also known in Italian as Giulio Schiavetto. He wrote collections of madrigals and motets between 1557 and 1573 while director of the choir in Sibenik Cathedral, in the town of Šibenik in Dalmatia. They are highly regarded today as examples of Renaissance music. Another period composer whose career stemmed from his work in the church was Ivan Lukačić (1584–1648), conductor and organist in the Split Cathedral. Lukačić is also known today for his sacred motets.

By the 18th century, Dubrovnik was a republic run by families of nobles. One, the Sorkočević-Sorgo family, is also remembered today for its wonderful contributions to music. Luka Sorkočević (1734–89) is regarded as the composer of the first symphony written in Dubrovnik. His sister Elena Pučić-Sorkočević is believed to be the first woman composer in the city, while his son Antun Sorkočević composed four symphonies and many pieces for chamber groups.

THREE CENTURIES, TWO GUITARISTS

In the 19th century, when people living in central Europe wanted to listen to the best guitarist alive, they went to hear a man named Ivan Padovec (1800–73). Born in the northern Croatian city of Varaždin, Ivan hoped to become a teacher, but while visiting an uncle in Austria, Ivan attended a concert given by a masterful Italian guitarist named Mauro Giuliani. He was so intrigued by the sound of the guitar, he decided right away to learn how to play it. He began teaching himself, using established guitarists as models.

At age 19 Padovec moved to Zagreb to attend a normal school and still planned a career as a teacher. After hearing repeated praise for his musical talents, Padovec dropped the idea of teaching and devoted his life to becoming a full-time musician. After taking formal lessons for the first time, Padovec started to perform in public, first giving concerts in 1827 throughout Croatia. In 1829 he settled in the big city of Vienna, Austria, where he played for the Royal Court. For most of the next few decades he composed and performed in the cultural capitals of Europe, including Prague, Frankfurt, and London. When Padovec performed in Zagreb in 1840, one music critic wrote, "Our particular attention was caught by our countryman Mr. Padovec, the composer and the best guitar virtuoso, who was not deprived at praise by even the severe critics in Vienna."

In middle age Padovec lost his eyesight—repercussions from a childhood accident. Lacking sight, he could no longer write or teach. Padovec continued to perform but did not earn enough money to support himself. In 1848 he moved in with his sister's family but in his later years lived in extreme poverty.

Strings

Orchestras and chamber groups aside, some of Croatia's finest musicians have favored stringed instruments for centuries. Historic records show that stringed instruments have existed in the region since around 300 B.C. What could be regarded as the national folk instrument of Croatia, the *tamburitza*, is related to the Italian mandolin and to the Russian folk

---

Padovec gave the last performance of his life in his hometown of Varaždin in 1871. A critic covering the concert wrote, "Just like a candle which gathers its strength and flames up, before finally going out, the weak, vulnerable old man gathered all his strength and gave his final concert last year in the Varazdin Theatre."

Ivan Padovec died on November 4, 1871. His legacy included 200 compositions.

Padovec's equal today might very well be a young woman named Ana Vidović (1980–   ). In 1993, at the age of 13, Vidović enrolled at the Zagreb Music Academy, becoming the school's youngest student ever. The next year she stunned the music critics of Europe by winning first prize at the prestigious Albert Augustine Memorial International Guitar Competition in Bath, England, where classical guitarists vie for honors. A music critic from the *Guitar Review*, John W. Duarte, wrote of Vidović, "Her technique was flawless, her mien was relaxed and modest, and the maturity of her musicality entirely belied her age—a mere 14 years. Neither the jury nor the audience could quite believe what they heard. A fellow juror not noted for his 'over-the-top' assessments said to me: 'We're privileged to have been here at the beginning of this girl's career'—and that about summed it up."

Since then, Vidović has won numerous other competitions, including Italy's Mauro Giuliani Competition, named for the master guitarist who so impressed Ivan Padovec over a century and a half earlier. Just in her early 20s, Vidović has recorded five compact discs and played either solo or with orchestras in over 20 countries, packing concert halls in world capitals including New York, London, Paris, Tel Aviv, Rome, and Toronto.

instrument called the balalaika, which has a long neck, a triangular body, and three strings. The *tamburitza* also has a long neck, but with an egg-shaped body, and is believed to have been invented over 700 years ago. *Tamburitzas* have various numbers of strings, ranging from two single strings to three courses of double strings, depending on the context in which they will be played.

The skills to play the *tamburitza* are passed down from one generation to the next. It was first played as a solo instrument, but in 1847, the first *tamburitzan* orchestra was formed in the city of Osijek, near the Serbian border. In 1882, the debut *tamburitzan* choir was started by a musician named Mijo Majer, the first arranger and composer for *tamburitzan* orchestras. Before long, *tamburitzan* orchestras and choirs were springing up not only in the Balkans but in Austria and Czechoslovakia, too. The premier *tamburitza* concert in the United States took place in 1900 in New York City's Carnegie Hall, and a few years later an American-Croatian *tamburitzan* orchestra played in the White House for President Theodore Roosevelt.

The instrument grew even more popular. In 1941, the Croatian Radio-Television Tamburitza Orchestra was formed as a house band for the Zagreb-based radio station. In 1960, Croatian-Americans in Pittsburgh, Pennsylvania, founded their own Tamburitza Philharmonic Orchestra, which consisted of 75 players. For Croats who live abroad, the instrument is a cultural symbol of their homeland.

The *tamburitza* is not the only popular stringed instrument in Croatia. During the 17th century an ancestor of the modern guitar was first heard in Croatia. It was used initially as an accompanying instrument, then as a solo one, and was especially popular in Dalmatia. By the mid-19th century the guitar was frequently played in Croatia in both classical and folk styles.

Rock

Not all Croatia's guitarists lean toward classical music. Croatia has had a vibrant rock music scene since 1963, when a Zagreb-based band called Crveni Koralji (The Red Corals) released its first single. For the next few years, Croatian rock bands recorded mostly cover versions of American or British songs in the Croatian language, but by the late 1960s Croatian bands such as Delfini and the Five Up began writing their own music. In 1968, a folk rock band from Zagreb, Grupa 220 (Group 220), became the first Croatian rock band to release an album with only their own material.

Among the most popular Croatian bands today are a veteran group formed in 1984 named Majke (Mothers). They began as a punk band but have in recent years gravitated toward a southern boogie sound, popularized in the United States by bands such as Lynyrd Skynyrd and the Allman Brothers Band. Another band which rode in on the punk wave is Krampusi, from Bjelovar, near the Hungarian border. The name Krampusi is based in the Croat word *krampus*, described as a fairy tale devil. The Bambi Molesters are an instrumental quartet whose roots are in early California surf music, Darkendome is one of the premier heavy metal bands, and Parni Valjak has been one of Croatia's most listened to mainstream rock and roll bands since they formed in 1988.

Art

As might be expected, the beginnings of Croatian art formed around the Catholic Church. Most of the earliest examples relate more to architecture than art. There are about 15 early medieval churches found along the Adriatic coast, dating from the ninth to 11th centuries. A classic example is the Church of the Holy Cross in Nin (ninth century), which is a typical Dalmatian church in the style called pre-Romanesque, with a cross-like ground plan, two small apses on the arms, and a squatty dome shaped like a silo.

The first Croatian artist of note was known simply as Radovan, or Master Radovan, whose name is roughly translated as "the joyous one." Born in the 13th century, he was a sculptor from Trogir, a small island off the coast of Split. One of Radovan's masterpieces is the portal of the cathedral in Split, adorned with a realistic image of Eve and with allegorical depictions of animals such as dogs and pigs.

Some of Croatia's Renaissance period artists are also best known for their religious-themed work. Vincent of Kastav and Ivan of Kastav, two

TWO ARTISTS NAMED IVAN

Ivan Generalić was born in the village of Hlebine in Croatia's north-eastern plains near the Drava River. He first made a name for himself at the tender age of 17 with his work at the 1931 exhibit at Zagreb's Art Pavilion. Due to his prominent role in the exhibit, Generalić is known as the father of Croatian naïve art. He became so identified with naïve art that he and his contemporaries became known as the Hlebine School, after Generalić's birthplace. He expressed his ideas in all sorts of media, including etchings, oil on wood or linen, and aquarelles (transparent watercolors).

In the years after World War II, Generalić shied away from social commentary in his art in favor of country landscapes. He mastered a technique of oil on glass and relied heavily on sophisticated shades of color. After 1970, at the age of 56, he changed his style once more, depicting existential and symbolic subjects with many paintings consisting entirely of one color. One of his most highly regarded from that period, *Sunflower*, depicts four sunflowers, with two enormous ones fronting a dark sky. Generalić died in the northern Croatian town of Koprivnica on November 27, 1992.

Ivan Meštrović, born in 1883, grew up in a peasant village named Otavice. His father was a farmer and was said to be the only literate man in town. Ivan's mother recited Gospel texts from memory, and her stories inspired him to carve Gospel heroes in wood and stone. When he was 16, Pavle Bilinić, a stonecutter in town, noticed the budding sculptor and invited him to live in his workshop in Split. Meštrović attended art school in Vienna and had his first exhibit there in 1905. His first big sale came not long afterward when the Austrian emperor purchased a Meštrović sculpture called *Mother and Child* that he had seen at an exhibition in Zagreb.

Meštrović moved to Rome and won worldwide respect after he took the first place for sculpture at an international exhibit there in 1911. The winning work depicted the heroes of the 1389 Kosovo battle as symbols of the patriotism and pride of the southern Slavic people. After all, this period just before the onset of World War I was a time of rebellion against the rule of Austria-Hungary. One critic made the claim that Meštrović was the greatest sculptor since the Renaissance.

Because of his political activism, Meštrović was forced to live in exile in Italy during World War I. Following the war, he returned to Yugoslavia and kept busy with one commission after another. A devout Catholic, he

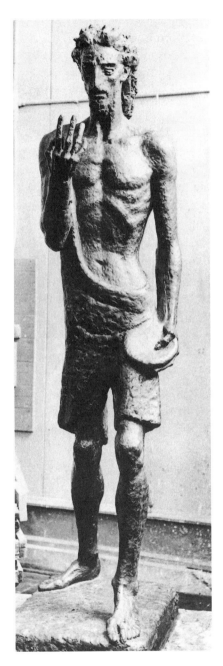

built numerous churches and statuary in his spare time which he donated. During World War II, he was an outspoken critic of Ante Pavelić's fascist government, for which he was duly punished with a prison sentence. Only negotiations by friends through the Vatican got him released after serving many months.

After the war, Meštrović moved to the United States, where he served as a professor at Syracuse University in upstate New York. By then he had turned away from political art, focusing on the tragedy of war and the hope of religious faith. Meštrović became a U.S. citizen in 1954 at a special ceremony conducted by President Eisenhower at the White House. He lived the rest of his life in the United States, moving to South Bend, Indiana, in 1955, but he never forgot his homeland. Late in his life the sculptor arranged for 59 of his statues to be delivered from the United States to Yugoslavia. Meštrović worked until his death in 1962.

St. John the Baptist *by Ivan Meštrović* (Courtesy Free Library of Philadelphia) painters who lived in the 15th century, were highly regarded for their frescoes in churches on the Istrian Peninsula. On the other hand, a sculptor named Frano Laurana (1420–1502), born in the Croatian town of Zadar, made his career in Italy sculpting busts of women. He is regarded as among the best of his period, a time when Renaissance art was at its peak. His work can be seen today in museums in cities such as Vienna, Paris, and New York.

Zadar was the birthplace of one other admired Croatian artist, Andrija Medulić (1500–63). Medulić was an important influence on two illustrious artists: the Italian painter Tintoretto, whose work includes St. George and the Dragon, and the Spanish painter El Greco.

Modern art in Croatia is said to have been born with the work of Vjekoslav Karas (1821–58). He painted with watercolors and oils and is remembered for his insightful portraits, including Roman Lady with Lute, dated between 1845 and 1847, which is part of the collection of the National Museum in Zagreb. It is a haunting work, depicting a dark-haired young woman in half profile looking pensively to the left. She wears a Roman town dress and sits in a black chair holding a lute in her lap.

After Karas, one of the most outstanding 19th-century Croatian painters was Vlaho Bukovac (1855–1922), son of an Italian father and Croatian mother. A native of the village of Cavtat, near Dubrovnik, Bukovac began his career in Paris in the late 1870s, concentrating on portraits. He gradually moved from traditional works to impressionism, and when he moved to Zagreb in 1894 he brought some lively artistic ideas to the local community. He spent the last 19 years of his life in Prague.

The biggest artistic movement in the 20th century in Croatia has been labeled naive art. Art historians say the movement came to life on September 13, 1931, when a group of painters known as the Zemlja (meaning "ground" or "soil") opened an exhibition at the Art Pavilion in Zagreb. The Zemlja consisted of peasants, and they produced what they considered art with a social purpose, which would serve the needs of the public and could be appreciated by anyone. Their works tend to be realistic and basic, with subjects ranging from still life to landscapes to religious images. One of the best known exhibits of Croatian naïve art was presented at the Ulrich Gallery in Zagreb on May 18, 1936. It consisted of the creations of three artists, the most prominent being Ivan Generalić (1914–92).

Aside from Generalić, the other most important Croatian artist of the 20th century was Ivan Mestrović (1883–1962). Unlike Generalić, Meštrović expressed himself as a sculptor.

Two other Croatian 20th-century artists who deserve mention are sculptor Antun Augustinčić (1900–79) and graphic artist Vrigilije Nevjestić. One of Augustinčić's best-known works, *Horsewoman (The Monument of Peace)*, can be seen by anyone visiting United Nations Headquarters in New York City, where it sits in front of the UN's home. Nevjestić's work can be best categorized as avant-garde. It belongs to numerous private collections, including that of former president of France Georges Pompidou. Nevjestić's most famous large work is titled *Vukovar*, which he called "a scream, a revolt against evil done to the Croatian people."

Film

Although Croatia has a small but vibrant film industry and has several award-winning filmmakers to its credit, Croatian movies seem to get little attention outside eastern Europe. However, one genre of the cinema industry has been the exception to this lack of publicity: animation.

Croatian cartoons are not just a laughing matter. The late 1950s and the early 1960s are said to be the golden age of Croatian animation, when Croatian cartoons won awards and respect throughout the world. However, the Croatian animation industry dates back much further. Animation studios in Zagreb first produced cartoons in the 1920s, not much later than the famed Hollywood studios did. By the 1930s Croatian animation was already world famous, but it was in the 1950s when the group of cartoonists known as the Zagreb School of Animated Film, or the Zagreb School of Cartoonists, truly excelled.

Ronald Holloway, a noted authority on European cinema, wrote, "The Zagreb School isn't a 'School' but a family. Perhaps nowhere else existed such a friendly atmosphere of mutual trust. . . . The artists met in a café in the courtyard of the old Zagreb Studios. That's where they came up with their best ideas. . . . In spite of tempting offers from other countries they were always drawn back home, to an atmosphere of freedom where they could freely exchange ideas and seek help when they needed it."

Unlike American animators and their fanciful cartoons directed toward children, the Zagreb cartoonists were known for short and concise animated films that took on the problems of adults in the real world. Much of their work was political, and they thought nothing of taking comedic shots at Titoism. Yugoslav animators would say to residents of other communist nations, "You are a product of Marxism, but we are descendants of the Marx Brothers," referring to the classic American comedy team of Groucho, Chico, and Harpo Marx, whose outrageous antics with their underlying social satire dominated the United States film comedy genre in the early 20th century.

Drawing styles have ranged from primitive, with characters who were little more than stick figures, to elaborate and lavish with backgrounds fronted by highly detailed characters. The animated short *Surogat (The Ersatz)*, created by Dušan Vukotić in 1961, was the first non-American film ever to win an Academy Award. The film lasts only nine minutes and features a tourist on a beach inflating an entire world.

In the late 1960s, based upon the stellar reputation of the Zagreb School of Animated Film, a group called the International Association of Animated Film (ASIFA) permitted the city of Zagreb to hold a biannual international festival of animated film. Zagreb's first such festival took place in June 1972, and since then, it has occurred every other spring.

The event has always been funded by the city of Zagreb and the Republic of Croatia, even when Croatia was a part of Yugoslavia, and the members of the Zagreb School of Animated Film have exclusively been responsible for lining up the animated films to be screened. In addition to screening films, festival goers get to hear talks from some of the world's legendary animators. Past speakers have included American cartoonists Friz Freleng (1905–95) and Chuck Jones (1912–2002), who for decades drew Warner Brothers cartoons featuring Porky Pig, Bugs Bunny, and Daffy Duck. William Hanna (1910–2001) has also appeared, as well as

The official poster of Zagreb Animafest 1990, designed by Ivan D'Roko
(Courtesy Zagreb Animafest)

Joseph Barbera, (1911–), whose studios created The Flintstones, Scooby Doo, and Ed, Edd, and Eddy.

Live-Action Film

Even though Croatia has had a live-action film industry since the earliest years of the 20th century, it was always overshadowed by the republic's animation business. There were, however, several important films made by Croatian directors and casts in the 1960s. One classic is a cerebral drama titled *Rondo,* directed by screenwriter Zvonimir Berković and released in 1966. It centers on a relationship between a married sculptor named Fedja and a single judge named Mladen, two friends who play chess every Sunday. Over time Mladen falls in love and has an illicit affair with Fedja's wife. The movie's focus is on the chessboard, with each move representing the emotions felt by the main characters.

Another noted movie from the era, *Lisice* (Handcuffs; 1969), had a sociopolitical theme: man's inhumanity to man. The conflict is set when in a small town a wedding procession is interrupted by two executioners looking for sympathizers of Soviet dictator Joseph Stalin, which begins the town's spiral into deadly chaos. Director Krsto Papić made a worldwide reputation for himself with this film.

A film themed similarly was *Kaja, Ubit ču Te* (Kaja, I'll kill you), directed by Vatroslav Mimica, in which the takeover of a peaceful Dalmatian town by fascists turns friend against friend. The title comes from a line in the film. Kaja, a common shopkeeper, is confronted in his store by a former friend, now a fascist sympathizer, who declares that not only are they no longer friends, but that he will now kill Kaja.

The War and Film

The war of the early 1990s has been fodder for young filmmakers, especially those who studied at the respected film department of the Zagreb Academy of Performing Arts. A woman named Jelena Rajković (1969–97) produced a superb documentary in 1992 about UNPRO-

FOR soldiers titled *Blue Helmet*. She followed that in 1995 with a suspenseful drama titled *Noc za slušanje* (A night for listening), about an armed war veteran who takes a radio station staff hostage until he is permitted to refute newspaper reports about his supposed death. Her dramatic film was broadcast on Croatian television, and curiously, a similar real life event took place at a real Croatian radio station the next day. Rajković then made a documentary about the bizarre but true event, which he completed in 1997 on the same day she died, at age 28, of an incurable disease.

One budding filmmaker named Lukas Nola (1964–) served as a military policeman during the war when air alerts were filling Zagreb with tension. Using his experiences, he wrote and directed an award-winning movie in 1994 titled *Svaki put kad se rastajemo* (Every time we part). In it Nola presents the war from the point of view of two refugees in Zagreb, a man and his daughter who escaped Slavonia after their house was burned and his wife was brutally murdered.

Another filmmaker, Vinko Brešan (1964–), used comedy to depict the senselessness of war in a 1996 film titled *Kako je počeo rat na mome okotu* (How the war started on my island). In the film, which Brešan wrote with his father, an established comedy writer named Ivo Brešan, the residents of an unnamed Dalmatian island want to strike a bargain with the Serb military occupiers. The residents will allow them to leave in peace if they will just leave. The commanding officer, Major Aleksa, refuses unless he receives an order from his superior. In one of the film's most memorable lines, Aleksa's wife urges him to agree, pleading, "Aleksa, come back home! I cooked pasta for you!" Still, Aleksa stubbornly refuses to give up. Finally, a soldier's father dresses in a military uniform pretending to be a colonel and orders Aleksa to leave. He finally does so. Brešan's movie was widely applauded by critics for combining humor and suspense to make a truly riveting film.

Literature

Written works dating to the 11th century relating to the Catholic Church have been found in Croatia, but the person regarded today as the first great writer from Croatia is Marko Marulić (1450–1524). He was born in Split and was heavily influenced by his main teacher, an Italian poet named Tideo Acciarini. Acciarini was a devoutly religious man who wrote in Latin. Marulić also wrote in Latin about mainly religious subjects.

Marulić wrote moralistic books, such as *Quinquaginta parabolae* in 1510, telling allegorical stories from the points of view of everyday working people such as fishermen and farmers. However, he is mostly identified by scholars today with an epic poem titled *Judita* (Judith), written in 1521. *Judita* tells the story of war between the Croats and Turks.

A verse follows:

As they walked, their legs slid about,
their steps were unsteady, their heads nodding;
their faces were red and noses damp,
on the hairs of their beards grease glistened.
Their swollen bellies protruded like pots,
their tongue cut words which they try to utter;
they made no sense, their eyes glittered,
they behaved badly, in the midst of laughter.

Marulić sprinkled his works with religious inspiration. In *Judita,* Marulić opines that with God's help the Croats will win. Marulić influenced huge numbers of younger Croatian poets including two named Petar Hektorović and Petar Zoranić, who publicly praised him in their own works.

For some time after the period when Marulić and his protégés shone, Croatian writers and poets were heavily influenced by those of Italy, but in the 19th century, with Slavic nationalism at its peak, Romanticism dominated Croatian literature. Poets such as Ivan Mažuranić and Stanko Vraž created patriotic poems filled with ideas of Slavic self-empowerment. Dimitrije Demeter wrote drama based on the same styles and ideas. A journalist, critic, and writer of historical novels, August Šenoa, emerged at that time and today ranks as one of the best Croatian novelists. A school of writers with a social conscience came out of the nationalist movement, including Vjenceslav

The silent companion keeping this reader company in a Zagreb park is a sculpture crafted in memory of poet Antun Gustav Matoš (1873–1914). The artist was Croatian sculptor Ivan Kožarić. (Courtesy United Nations)

Novak, Ante Kovacić, and Silvije Strahimir. They wrote about life among Croatia's lower classes.

Croatian literature of the 20th century was dominated by the works of one man, Miroslav Krleza (1893–1981). Born in Zagreb, Krleža started as a teenager writing poems filled with idealism and romanticism. World War I ruined his rosy outlook on life, and he began writing bitter antiwar essays and poems. He opposed the Yugoslav monarchy that emerged after the war, and in 1919 he founded a left-wing journal called *Plamen*. Impressed by the goals of the Bolsheviks, Krleža belonged to the Communist Party from 1918 to 1939.

One of his most admired works is a trilogy written between 1928 and 1932 about the fictional Glembay family, depicting the downfall of bourgeois society. However, perhaps his most respected creation is *Povratak Filipa Latinovića*, (The return of Philip Latinović), a 1932 morality tale about a Croatian artist who gives in to the corruption and dishonesty surrounding him.

In addition to his heavy-hitting comments on social issues, Krleza could paint a picture with his well-selected words. His book *Povratak Filipa Latinovicza* opens with the following: "It was dawn when Philip arrived at Kaptol railway station. For the last twenty-three years he had been away from this little backwater, but it was all still familiar to him: the rotting, slimy roofs, the round ball on the Friars' steeple, the grey windswept two-storied house at the end of the dark avenue, the plaster head of Medusa surmounting the heavy, iron-bound oak door with its cold latch."

While Krleza was a lifelong communist and supporter of Tito, he repeatedly criticized Stalin and his totalitarian regime. Because of that, his fellow communists never really trusted him.

NOTES

p. 100 "'Our particular attention was caught . . .'" Dojcinovic, Uros. "History of the Guitar in Former Yugoslavia," Guitarra Magazine website. Available on-line URL: http://www.guitarramagazine.com/issue42/guitar_yugoslav.asp. Downloaded on February 12, 2003.

p. 101 "'Just like a candle which gathers its strength . . .'" Dojcinovic, Uros. "History of the Guitar in Former Yugoslavia." Downloaded on February 12, 2003.

p. 101 "'We're privileged to have been here . . .'" Duarte, John W. "Croatia's Music Prodegy," Available on-line. URL: http://www.croatianmall.com/croatia/music/ana_vidovic.htm. Downloaded on February 12, 2003.

p. 104 "One critic made the claim that . . ." Croatia Net. "Ivan Mestrović," Croatia Net website. Available on-line. URL: http://www.croatia.net/html/mestrovic.html. Downloaded on February 11, 2003.

p. 107 "Nevjestić's most famous large work . . ." Zubrinic, Darko. "Art Overview," Croatia Net website. Available on-line. URL:http://www.croatia.net/html/art/html. Downloaded on February 11, 2003.

pp. 107–108 "'The Zagreb school isn't a . . .'" Petzke, Ingo. "40 Years of Animation made by Zagreb Film." Available on-line. URL: http://www.fh-wuerzburg.de/petzke/zagreb.html. Downloaded on February 15, 2003.

p. 108 "'You are a product of Marxism . . .'" Petzke, Ingo. "40 Years of Animation made by Zagreb Film." Downloaded on February 15, 2003.

p. 111 "'Aleksa, come back home! . . .'" Skrabalo, Ivo. "Young Croatian Film," *Central Europe Review,* October 25, 1999. Available on-line. URL: http://www.ce-review.org/99/18/kinoeye/18_skrabalo.html.Downloaded on February 15, 2003.

p. 112 "'As they walked, their legs slid about . . .'" Kadic, Ante. "Marko Marulic (1450–1524)," Croatia Net website. Available on-line. URL: http://www.croatia.net/html/marulic2.html. Downloaded on February 16, 2003.

p. 114 "'It was dawn when Philip arrived . . .'" Krleza Miroslav. *The Return of Philip Latinowicz.* (Evanston, Ill.: Northwestern University Press, 1995), p. 11.

8
DAILY LIFE

War has been over for years, but it still affects Croatians' daily routines. Just about every person in the republic was touched by the war in some way, and the populace is still very sensitive about it. Many have personal stories of heroism and tragedy, and just about all consider that there was only one correct side of the war—their side.

While life is not easy for Croatians, it is much worse in their neighboring republic of Bosnia and Herzegovina. Croatians have tried as hard as possible to get back into their normal routines of attending school, going to work, and making the most of their leisure hours. They celebrate holidays and have fun times with their friends and family.

Home Life

Croatian families are generally close knit. They are also usually paternal ones, but not necessarily as male-dominated as in some of the other former Yugoslav republics. There has been a considerable women's rights movement in Croatia since the mid-1970s, and it has challenged traditional cultural ideas regarding women's subservient roles both in the workplace and at home. Still, the kitchen is generally the center of the woman's realm at home. Nuclear families tend to be small, usually consisting of two parents and two to four children. It is not uncommon, though, for grandparents to spend their last years in their children's homes, where they can be looked after and can spend time playing with their grandchildren.

Urban housing differs considerably from that of Croatia's countryside. People in inner cities dwell mostly in older, single-family houses built from stone or in old apartment buildings. Small, single-family homes and modern high-rise apartments dominate city outskirts, while rural Croatia has small one- or two-story wooden homes with steep roofs and tidy little cabins or older whitewashed stone dwellings. In some of the newer countryside homes, especially those constructed after World War II, the dominant construction material is concrete.

Dress

Should you want to see lavish Croatian folk costumes, either buy a souvenir doll or visit on a holiday. At work, Croatians wear the same Western-style

Croats still dress in national costumes for folk dancing exhibitions on holidays or during festivals, such as this one in Dubrovnik. (Courtesy Croatian National Tourist Office, New York)

dress people wear in North America and the rest of Europe. People at work wear jackets and ties or dresses. Students or folks on a casual family outing can be seen in jeans, shorts, or tee shirts. Adults out for a night on the town tend toward the latest fashions from western Europe, which Croatians favor even though it might take months of scrimping and saving to buy them. Come on a holiday or festival, however, and you will be able to inspect women in traditional long, white linen dresses and brightly color fringed scarves and men in sheepskin coats or jerkins.

CROATIA'S CONTRIBUTION TO MEN'S WEAR

Every day, hundreds of millions of men across the world wear a Croatian invention to work, or perhaps out for an evening. It dates to the Thirty Years' War (1618–48), which was a religious-based series of wars fought between rival Catholics and Protestants throughout much of the European continent.

Some time during the war—the date has been estimated as anywhere from 1618 to 1635—a few thousand Croatian soldiers were brought in to fight on the side of France. The French were fascinated by scarves the Croatians wore as part of their military uniforms. Those worn by officers were made of cotton or silk, while the ones donned by common soldiers were crafted out of coarser materials.

On the other hand, French soldiers wore on their uniforms starched white lace collars, which were uncomfortable and awkward and much of the time were covered by the soldiers' long hair. The scarves the Croatians wore hung loosely, were easily seen, and needed much less care. French soldiers decided to do away with the collars and replace them with the Croatian-style scarves. By 1650 the unusual Croatian scarves were accepted by the royal court of France's King Louis XIV. Returning to England from exile in France, King Charles II brought the scarves with him. Within a decade they had swept Europe.

French men referred to wearing the new Croatian scarf as *a la croate*. That gradually evolved into *la cravate*. Today, the word *cravat* is still used to describe this men's fashion accessory. In the United States, it is known by another name, the necktie, and it is still in style over 350 years later.

Food

Croatians love food, especially meats such as pork, beef, and venison, and rich desserts. They savor dining with friends, especially in restaurants.

Croatians do not take breakfasts except to feed their children. If they do indulge it is usually in something light such as a small helping of burek, a layered pie stuffed with meat or cheese, and a tiny cup of strong coffee, usually espresso. Kids will grab a slice of bread, which they might top with butter, jam, or cheese, or sometimes cold cuts such as salami.

Lunch is the heavy meal of the day. It might start with a hearty bowl of soup, often lamb or potato, and follow with a full helping of a meat, a starch, and a salad.

Geography and history in Croatia dictate gastronomic tastes. Centuries of Hungarian rule left an epicurean legacy of goulash and paprikash (a meat stew), which have become staples in inland Croatia. Grapevines growing on Adriatic islands, including Hvar, are a result of ancient Greek occupation. Reminders of Turkish influence include *sarma* (stuffed sauerkraut rolls), and Italy's preference for pasta and seafood is echoed in Dalmatia, just across the Adriatic Sea from Italy.

Main lunch courses anywhere along the Adriatic, from the Istrian Peninsula all the way to Dubrovnik, might consist of *prstaci* (shellfish and pasta), *brodet* (mixed fish stew with rice), and scampi. The southern Italian favorite, pizza, as well as pasta are also enjoyed here. In Istria, a local cannelloni concoction is made from sliced prosciutto ham, mushrooms, and cottage cheese. It is served not in traditional cannelloni tubes but as pancakes. Other much loved Dalmatian dishes are *pašticada* (beef stuffed with lard and roasted in wine and various spices) and smoked ham, often served in slices as an appetizer.

Inland residents from the Zagreb area in central Croatia who are not savoring goulash or paprikash can be seen at lunchtime enjoying other meat and calorie-heavy specialties such as steak à la Zagreb (veal stuffed with ham and cheese, then rolled in breadcrumbs and fried), cutlet la Zagorje (sausages, sauerkraut, and boiled potatoes), and veal Easter egg (veal and mushrooms cooked in a spicy tomato sauce). Nonmeat specialties in inland Croatia are *manistra od bobica* (bean and corn soup) and *štrukle* (cottage cheese rolls).

Meals in the Serb-dominated Slavonia region usually center around meat and freshwater fish such as pike and carp and are often served with pasta. Prepared dishes tend to be heavy on paprika; *kulen* is sausage flavored with paprika and is a popular local preference. All of Croatia indulges in venison. In Dalmatia it is served roasted or sautéed in a sauce made of vinegar, olive oil, and wine. Venison is prepared with a heavier cream sauce in inland communities.

The day's third meal, dinner, is light. It is also similar to breakfast in content, consisting often of cereal, yogurt, a piece or two of bread, or a sandwich. Of course, children in Croatia are like those anywhere else and tend to shun their parents' traditional prepared preferences in favor of perennial favorites such as pizza, spaghetti, and hamburgers.

Dessert and Drinks

It is hard for any dessert-lover to lose weight, but that is especially so in Croatia, where sweet and rich cakes and candies rule. Lunches can be finished off with any of a variety of cakes and other desserts. Locally baked specialties include a spice cake called *paprenjak*, which originated on the Adriatic island of Hvar; a walnut cake called *orahnjaea*; *puenica s makon*, a cake with poppy seeds; and *smokvenjak*, a confection made from dried figs. Cakes aside, a nutritionally empty but tasty dessert is *hrostule*, deep fried and similar in texture to doughnuts or fritters.

It is surprising to many outsiders that Croatia produces some of Europe's finest wines. Unlike those of France and Germany, they are not exported in high numbers and therefore are not as highly publicized. *Dingač* is a thick red wine with about 15 to 16 percent alcohol and is Croatia's trademark. There are wineries throughout the republic. Red wines are produced mainly along the Adriatic coast, and white wines are made in northern and eastern parts of the nation.

A curious Croatian custom is to mix varied wines with water. In southern Croatia the top choice is a heavy red wine called *bevanda*; in the north it is a tart wine called *gemist*, which is weakened with mineral water. In addition to wines, top quality brandies, liqueurs, and beers are produced throughout Croatia.

Education

Croatians take the education of their children very seriously, and this emphasis on learning has a long history. In the 10th century, Croatia's first king, Tomislav, urged his subjects to permit their children to attend school so that they might become religious leaders. Today the republic boasts a literacy rate of 97 percent. As in the majority of nations, compulsory education for children between ages seven and 15 is free. However, in Croatia preschool education for youngsters ages three through six is also free.

Primary school lasts from ages seven through 11, while secondary school, also available for free, lasts for eight years in two periods, from ages 11–15 and 15–19. In their first years of school, children learn the same basics as in other countries, such as science, arithmetic, and reading. In fifth grade they begin foreign language studies. Students can get into serious trouble for not being well behaved in class. Every morning students must open their classroom doors for their teachers and are not permitted to sit before their teacher does.

Secondary education comes in numerous forms, including grammar schools, technical schools, and specialized schools. Children who are not of Croatian origin are provided special education in foreign languages, since members of all national ethnic minorities have the right to learn their minority language.

There are 86 colleges, universities, or other institutions of higher learning in Croatia, including polytechnic, maritime, and teachers' schools. However, with one out of five people of working age unemployed, many qualified youngsters do not get the chance to go to post–high school education. According to the 2001 census, just 5.85 percent of persons age 15 or older (198,000 of 1.55 million) have the equivalent of a college degree.

There is a total of four universities in the Republic of Croatia. Although the most highly respected is the University of Zagreb, the other three, widely spaced across the nation in Split, Osijek, and Rijeka, are also viewed as reputable institutions, and each has a long heritage.

The roots of the university system of Croatia date to 1396, when the republic's first institution for higher learning (a school for the study of theology) was founded by the Dominican order of the Catholic Church in Zadar, on the Dalmatian coast. It was initially called the College of Philosophy and Theology, and it had educated seminarians until it was closed in 1806 during Napoleon's occupation of Croatia. Zagreb's first such school, also an educational arm of the Catholic Church, was the Jesuit Academy in the royal free city of Zagreb, founded in 1669. Studies pertained mainly to theology, philosophy, and law.

Croatia's first modern university, which included more practical studies such as science and engineering, first admitted students in Zagreb in 1774. The person most credited for building the school was a maverick bishop and politician, Josip Juraj Strossmayer (1815–1905), who received worldwide attention among Catholics in 1869 when he gave a speech against the dogma of papal infallibility. Strossmayer was also known for his advocacy of a common homeland for southern Slavs.

The University of Zagreb today is a huge complex, with 25 separate colleges, about 3,000 professors and teaching assistants, and approximately 35,000 students. The university library, which dates to 1606, contains about 2.5 million books, and it is estimated that the university's dining halls serve students some 20,000 meals a day.

Croatia's Other Universities

The three other Croatian universities are considerably newer than the one in Zagreb but also have centuries-old ancestors. The University of Split, founded on June 15, 1974, sees its regional flavor as inspired by the College of Philosophy and Theology, founded up the coast in Zadar in 1396. The current university exploits its coastal location by offering studies in oceanography and fishery, island and coastal economy, regional tourism, nautical science, and naval architecture as well as traditional technical fields such as civil, mechanical, and electrical engineering.

The modern University of Rijeka, east of the Istrian Peninsula, dates to May 17, 1973, but it, too, claims a storied legacy. The Jesuits began the first institution of higher learning in Rijeka in 1627, and its theological facility came into existence in 1728. About 12,000 students annually attend the university, and there are about 860 teachers on staff.

The remaining university, in Osijek, near the Serbia border, is officially named the University J. J. Strossmayer in Osijek, after the bishop who laid the groundwork for the University of Zagreb in the 19th century. It traces its history to 1707, when the School of Higher Education in Philosophy was established in Osijek. Osijek's modern university was founded in 1975 and includes separate schools in all sorts of subjects, including economics, education, engineering, food technology, education, mathematics, agriculture, law, and medicine.

Holidays

Most of Croatia's national holidays revolve around the Catholic religion. They can be somewhat minor commemorations, such as St. Martin's Day on November 11, on which Croatians roast a goose for dinner and officially taste for the first time the season's new wine. All Saints Day, on November 1, is a time for memorials, when Croatian Catholics visit their family members' burial sites and light candles in their memories. The Feast of the Assumption and the Birth of the Virgin, on August 15, is observed by attending church and making pilgrimages. On Easter Sunday, Croatians attend church but also elaborately paint eggs with homemade dyes.

The Christmas season officially commences on December 6, St. Nicholas's Day. It is on this day, not Christmas morning, when children hang their stockings to be filled with all sorts of goodies. Bad youngsters do much worse than receive lumps of coal. They are warned that if they have not been on their good behavior they will be kidnapped by the devil Krampas and taken away in his bag.

A week later, on December 13, during the feast of St. Lucy, the mother of the family plants wheat grains. On Christmas Eve their green sprouts are tied with ribbons of the national colors: red, white, and blue. The family places three candies in the center of the sprouts, and this is used as a centerpiece on the family dining table. It stays there until Epiphany, on January 6. Croatians tend to wait until December 24 to decorate their Christmas trees. Some gifts are given on Christmas Day, but for the most part it is seen as a holy day for attending church, visiting with family, and wishing each other *Sretan Bozič,* or Merry Christmas.

Croatia's religious minorities celebrate their holidays as well. The Serb Orthodox Christmas is on January 7, and they also celebrate Easter on a different day than do Catholics. The most solemn holidays for Jews are Rosh Hashanah, the Jewish New Year, and Yom Kippur, the Day of Atonement, both taking place in early fall. Muslims' most important holiday is the month-long Ramadan, occurring during the ninth month of the Muslim calendar. Muslims fast during daylight hours during the entire month and eat small meals when it is dark outside.

The republic also has its share of national secular holidays. Labor Day takes place on May 1, Independence Day is May 30, Anti-Fascism Day is June 22, and Thanksgiving, or Gratitude Day, is August 5.

Sports

The favorite sports for Croatians to both play and watch are soccer and basketball. The first international soccer, or as it is called in Europe, football, match took place in 1907 against Chechnya. The Croatian Sporting

Children concentrate on getting the ball in an impromptu soccer match in Vukovar in eastern Croatia, oblivious to the damaged building behind them, a relic of years of war. (AP/Wide World Photos/Srdjan)

Union was formed just two years later. The two most popular soccer clubs are Croatia from Zagreb and Hajduk from Split. Croatia's national soccer team placed third in the 1998 World Cup.

Croatia's most successful basketball teams over the years have been Cibona from Zagreb and the former Jugoplastika from Split, both winners of numerous European tournaments. Several Croatian basketball players have gone on to careers in the National Basketball Association (NBA).

THREE GREAT ATHLETES

Dražen Petrović (1964–93) was one of the best shooting guards ever to play basketball in Europe and one of several Europeans good enough to play in the National Basketball Association (NBA). Basketball great Magic Johnson said of Petrović, "Dražen was one of the first guys who came from Europe who could get his shot off the dribble. He knew how to attack the basket, and he used his body so well. He opened the doors for the [European] guys who came behind him."

Born in the seaside town of Šibenik, Petrović began playing basketball as a child because his older brother Aleksander did. It became evident early on that he had raw talent, and he practiced every day before school. At age 15 he played for Šibenika, a team in the Yugoslav basketball first division. He followed his brother's steps, played for Cibona, and in his first year led his team to the European championship.

Petrović went on to play for two silver medal–winning Olympic teams (1988 and 1992). On one occasion he scored 112 points in a Croatian League game. In the late 1980s and early 1990s, Petrović played for the Portland Trail Blazers and the New Jersey Nets of the NBA, leading all NBA guards in field goal percentage in 1992, his final year with the Nets.

Petrović died in an automobile accident in 1993. In 2002, he was given the ultimate honor for any basketball player: election to the Basketball Hall of Fame in Springfield, Massachusetts.

Janica Kostelić (1982–   ) first stepped onto skis at age three outside her Zagreb home. Her mother, Mara, remembered, "She kept on falling and getting into the other children's way, and we thought she'd never learn how to ski."

(continues)

(continued)

Today, nobody has any questions about her skiing ability. Kostelić remembers starting serious training when she was about nine or 10 years old. A natural talent, she qualified to make the Croatian alpine skiing team at the 1988 Winter Olympics in Nagano, Japan, where she made news for being the youngest alpine skier at the event.

After competing and winning medals in several world cups, Kostelić became known in the world sports media as "the Croatian Sensation." Her story was especially compelling considering that Croatia was never regarded as a skiing powerhouse. While training in the resort town of St. Moritz, Switzerland, in the winter of 1999–2000, she took a brutal spill, injuring four ligaments in her right knee. Despite complicated surgery, doctors had doubts that she would ski competitively again.

Kostelić showed such concerns were unnecessary when she swept three gold medals in the 2002 Salt Lake City Winter Olympics in women's giant slalom, slalom, and combined. Then, in February 2003 she proved that her Salt Lake success was no fluke. She captured gold medals in women's giant slalom and combined in the World Alpine championships in St. Moritz. Her brother, Ivica Kostelić, captured the men's slalom in the same tournament. It was the first time siblings won the same event in the World Alpine championships.

Goran Ivanišević (1971–   ), a native of Split, first lifted a tennis racquet at age seven. Although he played soccer, basketball, and competed in cross-country races, Goran (named after his mother, Gorana) decided his career was in tennis. He turned pro at age 17 in 1988 and just two years later qualified for his first major grand slam tournament, the Australian Open, where he reached the quarter finals.

Although Ivanišević won several titles at smaller tennis tournaments throughout the 1990s, by the end of the decade he was known as the best player who never won a grand slam title. Ivanišević wanted especially to win Wimbledon. He had lost in three previous Wimbledon events: in 1992 to Andre Agassi, and in 1994 and 1998 to Pete Sampras. Finally, in 2001, after a long and strenuous battle, he beat Australian Pat Rafter in five sets: 6-3, 3-6, 6-3, 2-6, 9-7.

Ivanišević was not always gracious in his performance. He lost his temper on the court and insulted officials. With his bulging muscles, dark beard and mustache, and a garish tattoo of a cross, rose, and shark on his back, he was called by some the Croatian wild man, yet he impressed British Broadcasting Company sportscaster Rob Bonnet, who praised Ivanišević in a broadcast, saying,

I love him for the sheer purity of his ambition, the wonderment and joy he feels at his success, and his message that sport can utterly and absolutely fulfill. I love him for the contrast that he offers to Wimbledon and the stuffiness of its traditions. I love him for the genuine passion of his personality, for the love he shows to his native Croatia and for the courage which allows him to also love a Serb. . . .

Ivanišević was not finished making sports headlines. Although nursing an injured left shoulder, in February 2003 he stunned the tennis world by teaming with fellow Croat Ivan Ljubičić to come back from two sets down and beat the heavily favored United States players in that year's Davis Cup tournament.

Among the less publicized sports of which Croatians have excelled are handball and water polo, and their athletes have won many medals in the Olympics. Thanks to the over 20 mountains that reach higher than 1,000 meters (3,937 feet), the most popular individual participatory sports for Croatians are hiking, climbing, and mountaineering. A favorite training place for mountaineers is Anika Kuk rock, which stands at 700 meters (2,297 feet). Other sports enthusiasts perfect their skills in the fairly barren Velebit Mountains. One Croatian climber, Stipe Božić, did his training in his home country and later went on to climb Mount Everest on two occasions.

There are two other games popular in Croatia and hardly heard of anywhere else. One is *balote*, a kind of bowling played outdoors on a sandy rectangular field. It is mostly played leisurely on summer evenings by male amateurs. The other is *alka*, a sort of combination battle reenactment and war game. Based roughly on maneuvers of horse riding warriors in the Croatian defeat of the Turks in 1715, *alka* is officially played every August. Men called *Alkali* dress in traditional military uniforms and, while riding horseback, try to spear a lance through a line of rings hanging from a rope.

NOTES

p. 121 "In the 10th century, Croatia's . . ." *The World Almanac and Book of Facts 2003.* (New York: World Almanac Books, 2003), p. 776.

p. 121 "According to the 2001 census . . ." Croatian Bureau of Statistics. "Employed Persons aged 15 and over by age, sex, activity, and educational attainment, census 2001" Croatian Bureau of Statistics. Available on-line. URL:http://www.dzs.hr/Eng/Census/census2001.htm. Downloaded on February 17, 2003.

p. 122 "The university library . . ." Zubrinic, Darko. "University of Zagreb: A Short History of the University," University of Zagreb website. Available on-line. URL: http://www.hr/darko/etf/et2.html. Downloaded on February 14, 2003.

p. 125 "'Drazen was one of the first guys . . .'" Bogen, Mike. "Croatian legend honored at Hall," Springfield Union-News, September 27, 2002. Available on-lines. URL: http://www.masslive.com/printer/printer.ssf?/sports/pstories/sp928pet.html. Downloaded on September 28, 2002.

p. 125 "'She kept on falling and getting into . . .'" Janica website. "About Me," Janica Kostelić official website. Available on-line. URL: http://www.janica.hr/index.php?link=tko-sam-ja&lang=en. Downloaded on February 18, 2003.

p. 127 "'I love him for the sheer purity . . .'" Bonnet, Rob. "Rob Bonnet ponders the popularity of the new Wimbledon champ: Goran Ivanisevic," BBC Sport 2001, Goran Ivanisevic website. Available on-line. URL: http://www.goranonline.com/articles/gi_bbcsport-01.html. Downloaded on February 18, 2003.

9

CITIES

The cities of Croatia have been through a lot over the centuries. They have been devastated and rebuilt many times, and they have been ruled by so many different nations that many residents have lost track. Still, whether they are best known for camera-toting tourists or humming factories, the republic's big cities continue to thrive.

Zagreb

Zagreb is the political, cultural, and financial capital of Croatia. It is located in the north central part of the country on the banks of the Sava River, about 20 miles from the border with Slovenia. Zagreb, though hit by rockets during the war, did not suffer severe damage. More than 950,000 people live in Croatia's capital. Strolling through the city on an average day one will encounter local folk chain smoking as they dine in outdoor cafes, shopping for produce at the busy Dolac market downtown, taking in a basketball or soccer game, and commuting to work and home by car and by bus as well as by the ever popular tram system.

Zagreb is an anomaly among Europe's big cities in that it has not been discovered by Western tourists. Visitors to Croatia tend to congregate along the seacoast and in the eternal cities of Split and Dubrovnik. This lack of interaction with Western travelers has given Zagreb an image as a dowdy and unstylish city, yet to many inquisitive people, that is a plus.

Tourists from western Europe and North America are more likely to experience the true lifestyles of a big eastern European city that has had a minimum of outside influences.

The oldest existing records mentioning a community on the site of Zagreb date to 1094, when a bishopric was established there in what was then called Kaptol. The adjacent craftsmens' quarters were called Gradec. Zagreb gradually developed from these twin towns between

Zagreb, the capital of Croatia, owes its elegance to architecture from the baroque, Neoclassical, and Secessionist periods. The neo-baroque Croatian National Theater was built in the 19th century. (Courtesy Croatian National Tourist Office, New York)

the 1100s and the 1300s, both communities centered around Catholic churches: St. Stephen's Cathedral in Kaptol and St. Mark's Church in Gradec.

Visitors come to Zagreb today to see the remnants of both churches. The modern structure of St. Stephen's Cathedral has 13th-century frescoes (see chapter 6). The Gothic-style St. Mark's Church is best known for its multicolored painted tile roof depicting the coats of arms of Croatia, Dalmatia, Slavonia, and Zagreb. Inside St. Mark's are the works of sculptor Ivan Meštrović, while on the eastern side is the building housing the Sabor.

Those western tourists who have yet to discover Zagreb are in for a cultural bonanza should they ever set foot in the city. The people of Zagreb are proud of their museums and parks, and an enjoyable day can be had by looking at the best works of both man and nature.

One of the best and most underpublicized art museums in all of Europe is the Mimara Museum. It contains works by masters such as Rembrandt, Rubens, and Raphael as well as Egyptian antiquities, Oriental art, sculpture, and glassware. The museum, located in a former school building dating from 1883, grew out of an enormous collection donated by a Zagreb native named Ante Topić Mimara.

Another showcase for great works is the Strossmayer Gallery. Visitors whose tastes lean toward more recent creations can head to the Gallery of Modern Art. Zagreb also boasts the Museum of Arts and Crafts, containing everything from centuries-old clocks to a superb collection of Judaica. In the Archaeological Museum one can see both Egyptian mummies and a Roman sculpture garden. The Ethnographic Museum, founded in 1919 by a textile trader and manufacturer named Salomon Berger, is devoted to textiles and other folk art from Croatia.

Zagreb also has a busy nightlife. The Croatian National Theatre is the local venue for opera and ballet, while the Komedija Theatre stages operettas and musicals. Street performers are found in the flower market square known as Trg Petra Preradovića. Rock music can be heard on the streets called Tkalčićeva and Opatovina, where on Fridays and Saturdays young people club-hop and mingle outside. Should one think that Zagreb is all play, keep in mind that the city is also Croatia's main industrial center. Its factories manufacture textiles, machinery, paper, leather, and chemicals.

Split

The second-largest city in Croatia, Split is a world apart from Zagreb. Located a little over halfway down Croatia's Adriatic coastline in the heart of Dalmatia, with a population of about 190,000, Split is a resort city with a long heritage of shipbuilding. Indeed, shipbuilding today is one of the leading industries, along with manufacturing plastics, cement, and chemicals. A major hydroelectric power plant is also in the immediate vicinity. Split, known as Spalato in Italian, was settled in the late third century by Roman emperor Diocletian (245–313), who built a grand retirement palace of stone here between 295 and 305. Following his death, Roman rulers continued to use Diocletian's Palace as a retreat, but the city's population really took off in the seventh century when residents of the nearby colony of Salona sought a safe haven in the palace following war with a Balkan tribe called the Avars. Descendants of these Salonians still live in Split. At different times Split has been controlled by Venice, Austria, and, of course, Yugoslavia.

Vacationers come here for two main reasons. One is the seaside, which attracts boaters and sunbathers. Its oceanfront promenade is lined with palm trees, similar to what one might see in cities along the French Riviera. The other is the remains of Diocletian's Palace, regarded by experts as among the best preserved Roman-era ruins outside Italy. Interestingly, residents of ancient Split discarded what they considered trash in the palace rooms; this trash is now archaeologists' treasure and is on display in the complex. Other existing Roman ruins here include Diocletian's mausoleum, which was converted into a cathedral, and the baptistery, once a Roman temple. One other important sight in town is the Meštrović gallery, with a substantial collection of the artist's sculptures.

Zadar

Some travel experts say Zadar, located just north of Split, along the coast, is the most typical of Dalmatian cities. With a population of about 176,000, Zadar, like Split, is a seaport and resort center. As one might expect due to its seaside location, Zadar is home to a thriving processed seafood industry. It is also the location of factories producing cigarettes, textiles, and alcoholic beverages.

Like Split, Zadar claims a Roman heritage. However, Zadar's Roman ruins date back as far as the second century B.C., when it was established as a Roman colony. The remnants of a Roman forum from the colony's earliest days still exist, as does Trajan's Arch of Triumph. Trajan (53–117) was a Roman emperor known for constructing considerable monuments.

Zadar also claims the crown as the oldest Slavic town on the Adriatic. Evidence shows that South Slavs settled here as early as the sixth century. The most ancient Slavic structure in Zadar is St. Donat's Church, built early in the ninth century on the site of a Roman temple. Slabs of the original Roman structure can still be seen inside the church.

Because of its location on the Adriatic, Zadar has been a coveted community for as long as it has existed. It passed from the Roman to the Byzantine Empire in 553, and for much of the next several centuries was

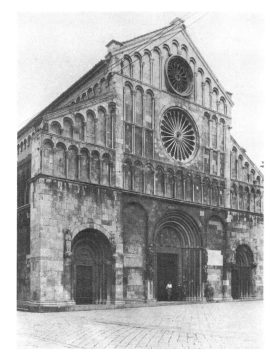

The cathedral in ancient Zadar (Courtesy Free Library of Philadelphia)

fought over by Venice, Hungary, and Croatia. Still, it officially remained part of the Byzantine empire until formally transferred to Venice in 1001.

Over the next 400 years Venice and Hungary fought continually over the city. Hungary claimed permanent possession of Zadar in 1409. During most of the 1800s, Zadar was part of the Austro-Hungarian Empire, and in 1919 it was declared part of Italy.

The twentieth century was not kind to Zadar. During World War II it was badly bombed by the Allies at war with Italy. Much of the historic center city was destroyed, and after Zadar was transferred to Yugoslavia in 1947 a significant effort was made to rebuild it in its native architectural style. History repeated itself in November 1991. This time the Serbs bombed the historic city center. They then controlled the community during a three-month-long siege. The important Maslenica Bridge, part of a main thoroughfare along the coast, was bombed and destroyed, then replaced by a pontoon bridge. Zadar was finally liberated by the Croats in January 1993, but because of those months of terror, many residents of Zadar are still bitter and suspicious of outsiders. However, little physical evidence of the fighting of the 1990s exists today.

Rijeka

Rijeka, with a population of about 168,000, is located at the junction of the Istrian Peninsula and the northern tip of Dalmatia in northwestern Croatia. Because of its location, it is a major transportation hub, with trains, ferries, and buses all stopping here en route to and from the big inland cities such as Zagreb and the coastal towns in Istria and Dalmatia. Its strategic site also makes Rijeka Croatia's largest port, and on any given day one will see in the harbor docked freighters, longshoremen and cranes continually loading cargo, and warehouses providing a home for surplus materials.

In addition to businesses relating to the shipping industry, Rijeka also has other important industries such as timber, pulp and paper, oil, and other petrochemical products. Mainly an industrial city—and according to some travel writers a grimy one—Rijeka draws few tourists except for those passing through to other destinations. However, like those of nearly all cities, Rijeka's officials yearn for tourist dollars. They promote its sunny climate, great for swimming and boating, and its modern art museum.

One interesting side note pertains to Rijeka's political location, near the border of Yugoslavia and Italy. From 1919 through 1945, the Italy-Yugoslavia border ran down the middle of the Rječina River through the city center.

Osijek

Osijek is the commercial and cultural center of Slavonia in easternmost Croatia. Located on the banks of the Drava River, this city of 130,000 has for much of its existence been a center of manufacturing. Many of the Osijek enterprises today were founded well over a century ago. One, a silk production company, actually began operation in 1774. Others include a match factory (founded in 1856), a tannery (1872), a furniture plant (1892), a sugar refinery (1905), a candy and chocolate factory (1907), and an ironworks (1912). Other major companies in Osijek manufacture textiles, leather goods, and agricultural machinery.

Like much of Croatia, Osijek dates to Roman times. In 331, Emperor Hadrian declared the ancient community of Mursa, the current site of Osijek, a colony with special privileges. The modern city of Osijek began growing around a castle built in 1091 atop the Roman ruins, and the first mention of Osijek is in a papal list of tithes from 1332. Under the Ottoman Empire, which ruled Osijek from 1526 to 1687, the famed Suleiman the Magnificent built a famous wooden bridge eight kilometers (roughly five miles) long and once said to be a wonder of the world. In 1786, three parts of the community, the Lower Town, Tvrdja, and the Upper Town were united into a major city, making Osijek the administrative capital of the Slavonia region. In the late 19th century it was part of Austria-Hungary before joining Yugoslavia.

Osijek was hit hard during the war years of the early 1990s. The Croatian National Theater, located in a building dating from 1866, was badly damaged in 1991 but has been rebuilt. One of the most engaging attractions for tourists is Tvrdja, Osijek's old town, with its many military buildings and baroque-style private residences.

Pula

Situated on the tip of the Istrian peninsula in northwestern Croatia, Pula, population about 62,000, has a superb geographical location and a lengthy heritage. In ancient Rome it was called Polensium. Its most commanding site today is the Roman amphitheater, which dates from the first century and overlooks the bustling harbor. Where as once the amphitheater was the site of gladiator matches, today it hosts rock concerts and a film festival every July.

Pula bursts with Roman antiquity. At the end of the busy street called Sergljevaca is the ancient forum, where one will also find the Temple of Augustus, said to be built between 2 B.C. and A.D. 14. Walk alongside the Roman walls that mark the town's original eastern boundary and one will encounter another period monument, the Triumphal Arch of Sergius, dating from A.D. 27 to 29. The city's Archaeological Museum of Istria showcases Pula's past from prehistory to medieval times, with a concentration on Roman stone artifacts.

The Roman amphitheater at Pula dates from the first century A.D. and is still in use today for performances and an annual film festival. (Courtesy Croatian National Tourist Office, New York)

From the Middle Ages through 1797, Venice possessed Pula. Buildings still standing from that period include the old town hall (1296), the Franciscan church (1314), and the museum of history, located in a Venetian citadel dating from the 17th century. Its curving medieval streets are a further remnant from that period. In 1797, Pula was transferred to Austria, and it became the main naval base of the Hapsburg Empire. Pula became part of Italy after World War I, and after World War II, part of Yugoslavia.

Like the Hapsburgs of old, today's Croatian leaders continue to take advantage of Pula's location by operating a naval base out of the city. It also has a busy commercial harbor with docks, shipyards, and related industries.

Šibenik

Another coastal city, Šibenik, or Sebenico in Italian, does not have the ancient heritage of other western Croatian towns and prides itself on that very fact. Home to about 42,000 people, Šibenik was founded in the 11th century by Croatian king Petar Krešimir IV. Today it boastfully claims itself as the oldest native Croatian town on the Adriatic Sea. Šibenik's early distinction was as the place of residence of Croatia's kings.

Located between Zadar and Split, Šibenik was conquered by Venice in 1117 and, except for the years 1351 to 1412, when Hungary controlled it, was part of the Venetian empire for well over six centuries. The Ottoman Turks tried many times to conquer Šibenik, often reaching the city's walls, but Venice never relinquished its control. Austria ruled Šibenik from 1797 to 1918, when it became a part the Kingdom of Serbs, Croats, and Slovenes.

Many Šibenik residents earn their living from the sea. The town is a port, navy base, and shipbuilding center. It also has metalworking and aluminum industries. Its most historic buildings were built during the Venetian period. These include the Cathedral of St. Jacob, raised between 1431 and 1455 and the symbol of the town, and the town hall, constructed in 1542. Šibenik also serves for nature-loving visitors as a base for two nearby national parks, preserving wilderness, waterfalls, and more than 100 ecologically-rich islands.

Dubrovnik

Storied Dubrovnik, the Pearl of the Adriatic and one of the world's best-loved tourist destinations, is actually a fairly small community, with only about 30,000 permanent residents. Dubrovnik was originally founded as a place of refuge around 700 by Romans escaping Slav invaders, but in time Slavs did settle in Dubrovnik, known through most of its existence by the name Ragusa, giving it a curious combination of Slavic and Italian influences.

Although Ragusa was for centuries technically a protectorate, or dependent region, of numerous empires including the Byzantines, Venice, Hungary, and the Ottomans, it was basically regarded as an independent merchant republic. That changed when in 1808 Ragusa was taken over by Napoleon and made part of the Illyrian provinces. In 1815, the Congress of Vienna turned the coastal city over to Austria, and in 1918 it became part of the Kingdom of Serbs, Croats, and Slovenes. It was also in 1918 that the city's name was changed to Dubrovnik.

Dubrovnik's beautifully preserved old town, known as Stari Grad, is surrounded by original stone city walls built mostly in the 1300s. The walls stretch over a mile and a half and are easily walked, interrupted by two round towers, 14 square towers, and a handful of fortifications. There are said to be few sunsets anywhere that are as spectacular as those seen from atop the walls overlooking the purplish-blue waters of the Adriatic.

Just about every structure in Stari Grad is made from the same light-colored stone, which is the basis for another of Dubrovnik's nicknames, The City Made of Stone and Light. Dubrovnik's museums, churches, palaces, and monuments are all crafted from the same stone. Contrasting with the main stone structures are vibrant tile roofs atop most of the town's buildings. When the architecture is combined with the natural setting, it is clear that Dubrovnik is one of the most dazzling and beautiful cities on the face of the earth.

The town fought for its survival in the war of the early 1990s. Dubrovnik was the scene of severe shelling during the siege by the Yugoslav army from October 1991 to May 1992. Some buildings and many of the town's distinctive tiled roofs, which had stood for centuries, were destroyed. After the war the town became part of a huge rebuilding

Jutting into the Adriatic, Dubrovnik is ranked as one of the world's most beautiful cities. (Courtesy Free Library of Philadelphia)

campaign, which has generally been accepted as successful. If you go to Dubrovnik today, the only visual evidence of the war is the bullet holes in buildings and new tiles in roofs that don't quite match the old ones. While Dubrovnik has an active port with some light industry, its main business is tourism, and the tourism industry has made a comeback since the war.

10

PRESENT PROBLEMS AND FUTURE SOLUTIONS

No nation is without problems, but a radical change in an economic system immediately followed by a bloody war and a long reconstruction process would test the resolve of the people of any country. War begets enduring problems, such as refugees who wish to return home, war criminals who should be brought to justice, and dangerous remnants of battle such as landmines, which need to be cleared. Of course, there is also the monumental task of improving the nation's economy.

The Positives

Despite all the turmoil Croatia has gone through since the early 1990s, peace exists in the republic today. It is certainly not accurate to say all is forgiven, and there is much bitterness on all sides. However, there is no more aggressive military action, nobody in Croatia is living under siege, and citizens can walk the streets without concern about being hit by an errant shell.

Although many people have wondered at times about the usefulness of the United Nations and NATO, it is clear that their endeavors in Croatia were successful. In addition, while the dust has yet to settle completely from the civil war, the battle-weary people of Croatia have shown their determination to do what they can to keep the peace.

Because Croatia was one of the more prosperous and industrialized regions of the former Yugoslavia, the nation's economy never hit the depths that other former republics did, such as Bosnia and Herzegovina. The end of the Tudjman administration and the election of Stipe Mesić helped Croatia's economy begin to climb out of a deep recession. On the other hand, Croatia's economy is hardly thriving.

Human Rights and Refugees

Only July 15, 2002, the heads of Croatia, Bosnia and Herzegovina, and what was then Yugoslavia met in Sarajevo in a historic conference, the first such get-together since the end of the civil war. They pledged to work together to rebuild peace in their region. Stipe Mesić announced, "We are three countries that emerged from the former Yugoslavia—countries that are now in transition and must cooperate with each other, because our economies depend on each other. . . . Behind us is a brutal war which has left heavy consequences. Europe is integrating and that's our destiny, too. We want to cooperate with Bosnia-Herzegovina and with Yugoslavia."

To be taken seriously in this regard, Croatia must be fair to its minority residents, and as good as Mesić's intentions may be, getting them to reach fruition is another story. According to a watchdog organization called Human Rights Watch (HRW), ensuring minority rights within its borders has been Croatia's biggest human rights challenge. The Croatian government has been weak in supporting the return of Croatian Serb refugees. At the end of 2002, the majority of the 350,000 displaced Croatian Serbs had not returned to their homes. According to the United Nations High Commissioner for Refugees (UNHCR), only about 110,000 have come back. Reasons range from the inability to find work, the discrimination against refugees, and the fact that their prewar homes no longer exist or are occupied by others.

The Sabor's efforts to help refugees have produced mixed messages. On the one hand, in December 2002 the Sabor adopted the new Constitutional Law on National Minorities, with the purpose of improving conditions for minority participation in public life on all levels. Still, many in the Sabor feel the Serbs' claims to lost property should be limited, and well into 2003 some members were introducing legislation reflecting those beliefs.

International and European bodies have urged Mesić to concentrate on resolving the refugee problem once and for all. Such pressure may have had an effect on Mesić. The fact that Croatia strongly wants membership in the EU can only help expedite its efforts in this regard. In March 2003, Mesić proposed to initiate a high-level meeting focusing on the return of refugees. The head of the Organization for Security and Cooperation in Europe (OSCE) immediately announced its support for such an idea. The head of the OSCE Mission to Croatia, Peter Semneby, stated, "This proposal is timely given Croatia's European Union membership application. . . . Strong political signals are required to enhance the public acceptance of refugee return. Essential aspects of that climate are also property restitution, reconstruction of destroyed houses and resolution of the occupancy/tenancy rights issue."

Alleged War Criminals

When the International Criminal Tribunal for the Former Yugoslavia was established, the idea was simple: Because there was a probability that individual nations would view suspected war criminals with prejudice, an independent body was needed to ensure that justice would prevail and true war criminals would be punished.

Nevertheless, there is an inherent problem with the system. The tribunal depends on nations voluntarily turning over their citizens who are suspected criminals. Croatia has drawn the wrath of the tribunal as well as other Balkan nations for what is perceived as its lack of cooperation in this matter. Officials of the EU have warned that Croatia will not be permitted to join the body until the republic cooperates better with the war crimes tribunal.

One case in point is that of General Janko Bobetko, a burly, bald-headed man who was indicted on September 20, 2002, on two counts of crimes against humanity and three counts of violations of the laws or customs of war. Specifically, Bobetko is charged with killing at least 100 Serb civilians during a battle on September 9, 1993, in a Serb-dominated part of Croatia known as the Medak Pocket. While he may not have actually taken part in the killings, tribunal prosecutors allege that he knew his troops were murdering Serb civilians and did nothing to either stop them or punish them afterward.

But to many Croatians, Bobetko is a war hero. He was Croatia's army chief of staff during the civil war, and polls indicate that 80 percent of Croatian citizens oppose turning Bobetko over to the tribunal. To them extraditing Bobetko would be equivalent to turning over an innocent man they are sure would not get a fair trial. Fearing possible pariah status, President Mesić, clearly in the minority, has begged the Sabor and Bobetko to cooperate with the tribunal.

Unfortunately, as with many international matters, political animosity plays a role here. During his trial on 66 counts of war crimes, former Yugoslav strongman Slobodan Milošević testified in October 2002 that Croatian president Mesić was himself guilty of similar crimes. Milošević accused Mesić of ordering the torching and destruction of Serb-dominated villages in Croatia. Mesić has not been charged and has emphatically denied Milošević's claims. Said Mesić, "This is a product of someone's fantasy. I had as much influence (on the men's murder) as I had on Lincoln's assassination."

Even so, Milošević's claim opens up the proverbial can of worms. Should his accusations be taken seriously, or are they the rants of a guilty man drawing attention away from himself to avoid conviction? If Mesić is not charged, will it look like the tribunal is playing favorites? If he is charged, would it look like the tribunal is appeasing the Serbs? And if so, what would happen to Croatia's stability? One can only hope that tribunal prosecutors will ignore politics and base charges solely on available evidence.

Land Mines

Among the most hotly debated military weapons are land mines, used liberally during the Balkan wars of the early 1990s. Many well-known activists, from military personnel to celebrities, have urged a worldwide ban on them. Two of the more outspoken are former member of the Beatles Paul McCartney and his wife, Heather Mills. At the 2001 opening of their nonprofit mine-clearance organization, Adopt-A-Minefield UK,

McCartney stated, "Imagine living in a country during a terrible war and then peace is declared. You think the killing is over, but when you take your kids to the beach you can't walk on it because the beach blows up if you do. This is the legacy of the land mine."

Croatia is said to be among the world's top 10 mine-infested nations. More than 1.5 million land mines were deployed in Croatia during the war. It is estimated that there have been between upwards of 1,800 land-mine victims in Croatia since 1991. Personal stories are heartbreaking. In March 1999, a farmer named Nikola Katić was plowing his land and accidentally drove his tractor over a land mine. After 12 days of suffering from his wounds, he died of his injuries. As a result of his death, today his family has no means of support. Another case took place in 1997 when a 72-year-old man named Stojan Radić was picking chestnuts in a forest near his house. He unknowingly stepped on a land mine, severely injuring a leg, which ultimately had to be amputated.

In 1997, Croatia set a goal of being land-mine free by 2020, but the Croatian Mine Action Center (CROMAC), the agency in charge of mine clearing, faces a mind boggling task in reaching that goal. The cost to clear an area the size of a soccer field is an exorbitant $50,000. The government has limited resources, and its top priority has been to clear residential areas, leaving large tracts of wilderness and agricultural land virtually untouched.

Help is coming from a variety of sources, including foreign government agencies and independent charities, such as McCartney's group. It has also come from some unlikely places. On February 13, 2003, the United States Tennis Association announced it would donate $25,000 to the eradication of land mines in the village of Mekusje, site of a once popular tennis court. That donation was immediately matched by the United States Department of State. The gift was inspired by the Davis Cup team's visit to a mine clearance operation in Croatia earlier in the month. The team was in Croatia for a Davis Cup competition.

Meanwhile, stopgap efforts are taking place while the tedious process of mine clearing continues. Areas believed to be mine-infested are being marked by signposts warning people to stay away. In addition, CROMAC is encouraging regional governments to devise lists of mine clearing priorities, so resources can be best allocated toward villages and towns where the need is greatest.

NOTES

p. 141 "'We are three countries that emerged . . .'" CNN. "Balkan heads vow to rebuild peace," CNN website, July 15, 2002. Available on-line. URL: http://www.cnn.com/2002/WORLD/europe/07/15/balkans.summit/index.html. Downloaded on March 8, 2003.

p. 141 "According to the United Nations High Commissioner . . ." Human Rights Watch World Report 2003. "Croatia: Human Rights Developments," Human Rights Watch website. Available on-line. URL: http://hrw.org/wr2k3/europe6.html. Downloaded on February 17, 2003.

p. 142 "'This proposal is timely . . .'" OSCE. "OSCE Mission supports Croatian President's initiative on refugee return," OSCE website, March 10, 2003, Available on-line. URL: http://www.reliefweb.int/w/rwb/nsf. . . . Downloaded on March 10, 2003.

p. 142 "Specifically, Bobetko is charged with . . ." United Nations. "Case Information Sheet: Bobetko Case (IR-02-62)," United Nations website, October 8, 2002. Available on-line. URL: http://www.un.org/icty/glance/bobetko.htm. Downloaded on March 10, 2003.

p. 143 "He was Croatia's army chief of staff . . ." British Broadcasting Corporation. "Croatia debates extradition crisis," BBC website, September 27, 2002. Available on-line. URL: http://news.bbc.co.uk/1/hi/world/Europe/2284638.stm. Downloaded on March 8, 2003.

p. 143 "'This is a product of someone's fantasy. . . .'" CNN. "Milošević grills Croat president," CNN website, October 2, 2002. Available on-line. URL: http://www.cnn.com/2002/WORLD/europe/10/02/milosevic/index.html. Downloaded on September 8, 2002.

p. 144 "'Imagine living in a country during a terrible war . . .'" CNN. "McCartney launches land mine campaign," CNN website, June 4, 2001. Available on-line. URL: http://www.cnn.com/2001/SHOWBIZ/Music/06/04/mccartney.mines/index.html. Downloaded on March 11, 2003.

p. 144 "More than 1.5 million land mines . . ." Prevendar, Marijana. "From the Field: Croatia," James Madison University Journal, November 1999. Available on-line. URL: http://maic.jmu.edu/journal/4.1/notes_croatia.htm. Downloaded on March 11, 2003.

p. 144 "It is estimated that . . ." Balkantimes.com. "Croatia Still Plagued by Land mines," Southeast European Times, 2002. Available on-line. URL: http://www.balkantimes.com. Downloaded on March 11, 2003.

CHRONOLOGY

1000 B.C.

First tribes migrate into Illyria, now Croatia

Fourth century B.C.

Greeks invade Illyria

Second century B.C.

Roman Empire extends into Dalmatia

9 B.C.

Under Emperor Augustus, Romans control all of Illyria

A.D. 400

First Croats enter Illyria

700s

Franks conquer Croats

924 or 925

Tomislav crowned first king of the Croats

1091

Hungarian King Laszlo I establishes bishopric in Zagreb

1102

Pacta Conventa signed between Hungary and Croatia

1420
Dalmatia comes under the control of the city-state Venice

1526
Ottoman Turks defeat Hungarians at Battle of Mohacs

1609
Croatian Sabor bans all religions other than Catholicism

1699
Nearly all of Croatia comes under Hapsburg rule

1765–80s
Emperor Joseph II takes Hapsburg throne, begins modernization of empire

Early 1800s
Napoleon conquers much of Europe including western Croatia

1832
Croatian nationalist movement begins

1866
Hapsburgs lose Battle of Königgrätz

1867
Croatia becomes part of Kingdom of Austria-Hungary

1868
Sabor adopts Nagodba giving Croatia limited autonomy

1881
Austria-Hungary extends military border into Serbia

1908
Croats and Serbs win majority in Sabor

1912–1914

Balkan wars; Archduke Francis Ferdinand of Austria-Hungary assassinated in Sarajevo, triggering World War I

1917

Corfu Declaration announced, with plans to form a pan-southern Slavic kingdom

1918

World War I ends; Serbian crown prince Alexander forms new nation: Kingdom of Serbs, Croats, and Slovenes

1921

Croats approve Constitution of the Neutral Peasant Republic of Croatia

1928

Stjepan Radić and two other Croat diplomats assassinated in Parliament in Belgrade

1929

Alexander names himself absolute ruler of the kingdom, renamed Yugoslavia (Kingdom of the South Slavs)

Early 1930s

Fascist Ustaša formed by Ante Pavelić

1934

Alexander assassinated by member of Ustaša

1935

Milan Stojadinović named prime minister by Prince Pavle

1936

Pavelić writes *The Croat Question*, outlining Ustaša's goals.

1939
Dragiša Cvetković named prime minister by Prince Pavle; World War II begins

1941
Nazi Germany attacks Yugoslavia two years into World War II; Yugoslavia surrenders; Nazis install Pavelić as head of the Independent State of Croatia

1941–45
Jews, Roma (Gypsies), and others sent to death camps

1943
Antifascist Council for the National Liberation of Yugoslavia, also known as the Partisans, meet in Jajce and make postwar plans

1945
Germany and Ustaša surrender; World War II ends; Tito takes over nation's leadership, employs liberalized form of communist government referred to as Titoism; Croatia again becomes a republic within Yugoslavia

1969–71
Croatian Spring reform movement

1980
Tito dies; system of rotating presidents takes effect

1983
Krajgher Commission Report released, calls for a form of free market economy in Yugoslavia

1984
Winter Olympics held in Sarajevo

1987
Agrokomerc scandal exposes widespread corruption in Yugoslavian business

1989
Major unrest with more than 1,900 labor strikes

1990
In first free elections in more than 50 years, League of Communists in Yugoslavia loses power to the Croatian Democratic Union (HDZ) led by Franjo Tudjman; Serbs in Serb-dominated areas of Croatia declare autonomy

1991
June 25: Croatia officially declares independence
October: Yugoslav People's Army (JNA) begins siege of Dubrovnik
November: Serbs and JNA control one third of Croatia

1992
January 2: JNA and Croatian National Guard sign unconditional cease fire
February: A total of 14,000 UNPROFOR troops arrive in Croatia
May: JNA begins withdrawal from Croatia; Croatia admitted into the United Nations; siege of Dubrovnik ends
September: Yugoslavia recognizes independent Croatia with conditions
October 24: Bosnian Croats proclaim Croatian Union of Herzeg-Bosna; Tudjman sends Croat troops into Bosnia

1993
May 25: International Criminal Tribunal for the former Yugoslavia is ratified by the United Nations Security Council
September: Muslims kill more than 35 Croat civilians in the town of Križ, Bosnia and Herzegovina
October 8: Croatian mass murder of Muslim civilians
November 9: Croatian soldiers destroy Mostar Bridge in Bosnia and Herzegovina

1994
March: Tudjman agrees to concept of Bosnia-Croat federation in Bosnia and Herzegovina

March 30: Cease-fire negotiated between Croatia and Croatian Serbs
October: Formation of Zagreb Group

1995

May 1–2: Heavy fighting between Croatia and Croatian Serbs over road access
August 4: Croatian troops invade Krajina
November 1: Peace talks begin at Wright-Patterson Air Force Base in Dayton, Ohio
November 12: Croatia and Eastern Slavonia sign treaty regarding reintegration of Croatian Serbs into Croatia
November 21: Peace treaty agreed upon in Dayton ends war
December 14: Peace treaty signed in Paris, France

1996

May: Croatian House of Representatives grants amnesty for many crimes committed during war

1997

April 13: The HDZ dominates parliamentary elections
June 15: Tudjman reelected president
June: First indictments for war crimes issued

1998

February: Civil unrest in Zagreb over poor postwar living conditions

1999

January: UNTAES mandate on Eastern Slavonia ends
Spring-summer: Tudjman's government attacked over human rights violations; Tudjman reorganizes government
December 10: Tudjman dies

2000

January 3: HDZ is big loser in parliamentary elections
February 7: Stipe Mesić elected president
November–Spring 2001: Series of amendments to constitution are enacted that limit presidential power and abolish Chamber of Counties

2001

May: Mesić government survives vote of confidence

2002

April: Croatia's and Serbia's foreign ministers meet

July: Prime Minister Ivica Račan resigns, Mesić government reorganized

September: Government refuses to extradite General Janko Bobetko to the International Criminal Tribunal for the Former Yugoslavia

2003

February: Croatia submits formal application for European Union membership

FURTHER READING

Bat-Ami, Miriam. *Two Suns in the Sky*. Chicago: Front Street/Cricket Books, 1999.

Bran, Zoe. *After Yugoslavia*. Oakland: Lonely Planet Publications, 2001.

Curtin, Leah. *Sunflowers in the Sand: Stories from Children of War*. Lanham, Md.: Madison Books, 1999.

Doder, Dusko, and Louise Bronson. *Milosevic: Portrait of a Tyrant*. New York: The Free Press, 1999.

Fearon, Globe. *Teenage Refugees from Bosnia-Herzegovina Speak Out*. New York: Rosen Publishing Group, 1997.

Filipovic, Zlata. *Zlata's Diary: A Child's Life in Sarajevo*. New York: Viking Press, 1994.

Grant, James P. *I Dream of Peace: Images of War by Children of Former Yugoslavia*. New York: HarperCollins, 1994.

Marcovitz, Hal. *The Balkans: People in Conflict*. Philadelphia: Chelsea House, 2002.

Mertis, Julie, et al. *The Suitcase: Refugee Voices from Bosnia and Croatia*. Berkeley: University of California Press, 1997.

Ousseimi, Maria. *Caught in the Crossfire: Growing Up in a War Zone*. New York: Walker & Co., 1995.

Owen, Luisa Lang. *Casualty of War: A Childhood Revealed*. College Station, Tex.: Texas A&M University, 2003.

Ricciuti, Edward. *War in Yugoslavia: The Breakup of a Nation*. Brookfield, Conn.: Millbrook Press, 1993.

Rieff, David, *Slaughterhouse: Bosnia and the Failure of the West*. New York: Simon & Schuster, 1995.

Silber, Laura. *Yugoslavia: Death of a Nation*. New York: Penguin Books, 1997.

Simoen, Jan. *What About Anna?* New York: Walker & Company, 2002.

Stallaerts, Robert, and Jeannine Laurens. *Historical Dictionary of the Republic of Croatia*. Metuchen, N.J.: The Scarecrow Press, Inc., 1995.

West, Dame Rebecca. *Black Lamb and Grey Falcon*. New York: Viking Press, 1943.

Woog, Adam. *The United Nations*. San Diego: Lucent Books, 1994.

INDEX